The HEALINGHEART

AN ILLUSTRATED HISTORY OF CARDIOLOGY

PRESENTED AS A SERVICE TO MEDICINE BY

 Bristol-Myers Squibb Company

"*Discovery follows discovery,
each both raising and
answering questions, each
ending a long search, and
each providing the new
instruments for a new search.*"

J. ROBERT OPPENHEIMER,
PROSPECTS IN THE ARTS AND SCIENCES, AN ESSAY

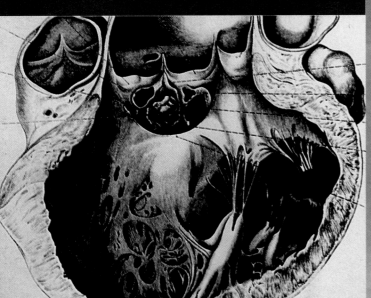

The HEALINGHEART

AN ILLUSTRATED HISTORY OF CARDIOLOGY

*W*ITH COMMENTARY BY

Wendy B. Murphy

GP **Greenwich Press**
Greenwich Connecticut

Greenwich Press
500 West Putnam Avenue
Greenwich, CT 06830

ISBN: 1-57013-070-1
Group Publisher: Corey Kupersmith, RPh
Publisher: Bradley Mock
Editorial Director: Lois Gandt
Manager, Editorial Services: Joanne King
Project Editor: Tammy Todaro
Copy Editor: Patrice Hibbard
Art Director: Jill Ruscoll
Assistant Art Director: Megan Rickards Youngquist
Designer: Jody Gross

Every effort has been made to ensure the medical and historical accuracy of this book. The author regrets any errors, either fact or omission.

Printed in the United States of America

Contents

Introduction

Westerners have long regarded the heart as being at the center of life, the so-called "vital principle," the place wherein passion dwells. But deep as man's appreciation and awe have been, the countless discoveries revealing how the heart and circulatory system actually work, and how best to intervene therapeutically when needed, are relatively recent phenomena.

Early thinkers were much better equipped philosophically and practically to turn their eyes to the heavens in search of cosmic discoveries than they were to look within. This is because the world of medicine was for so long dominated by Galenic doctrines, whose roots were in ancient magic and superstition rather than in observed physiology or biology. Indeed, for many centuries, the autopsies that could have revealed the most basic elements of human anatomy were forbidden by religious law.

Andreas Vesalius, a professor of anatomy at Padua, was the first to cross this great divide. Rejecting the musty lessons of his own teachers who, he claimed, had never used a knife except at the dinner table, Vesalius performed secret dissections on the bodies of executed prisoners to produce his revolutionary textbook on gross anatomy, *De Humani Corporis Fabrica* in 1543. Still, it was the rare physician who dared venture beyond to see how the heart heaved in the chest cavity or how it interacted with other organs of the body. Consequently, many of the most essential facts of physiology and pathology continued to be unknown, misunderstood, or overlooked altogether.

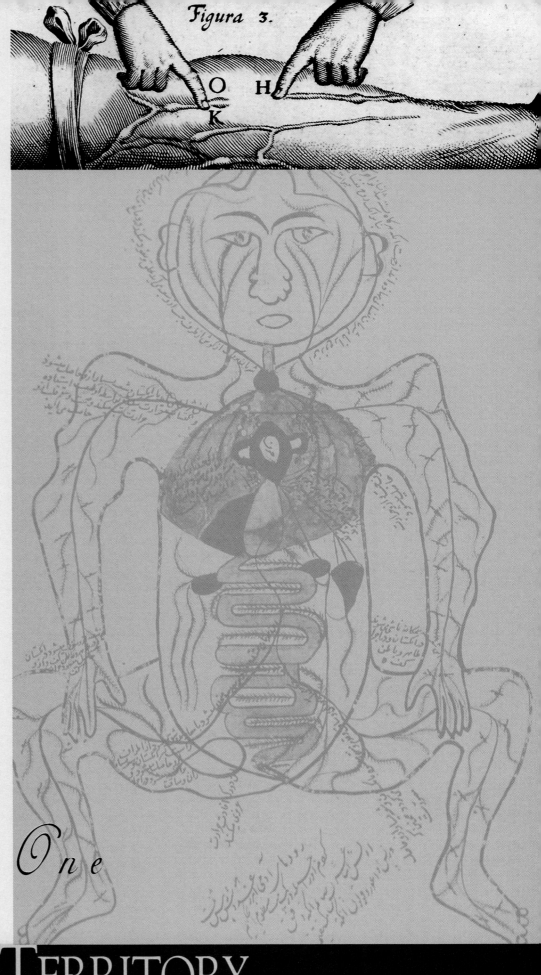

Figura 3.

O H
K

Chapter One

FORBIDDEN TERRITORY

Though the practice of medicine is very ancient, meaningful intervention in disorders and diseases of the heart is a relatively recent phenomenon, having developed only in the last century. For more than 2,000 years, the heart had been considered inviolable, because it was both the seat of the vital principle of life and an organ of extraordinary delicacy. In 350 BC, Aristotle, the Greek scholar whose influence long dominated Western science and philosophy, stated the practical side of the argument when he declared, "The heart alone of all the viscera cannot withstand injury."

As to what might go wrong with the heart and why, the ancient doctrine of humoral pathology provided the fundamentals. First described by the 5th century BC Greek physician Hippocrates and codified by Galen of Pergamum in the second century AD, this doctrine held that man's health as well as his temperament were determined by the four bodily fluids or "humors"—blood, phlegm, black bile, and yellow bile. Galen's interpretation of the role of the heart is particularly interesting. He postulated that, in addition to the four humors, three "pneuma" or spirits were at work. Accordingly, he conceived that blood was formed in the liver from food absorbed through the intestines and that the liver's own "natural spirit" combined with nutrients to form venous blood. This blood then flowed into the right ventricle, some of it going from there to nourish the lungs, but the majority being shunted through "invisible pores" in the ventricle to enter the left chamber. Here it was charged with "vital spirit."

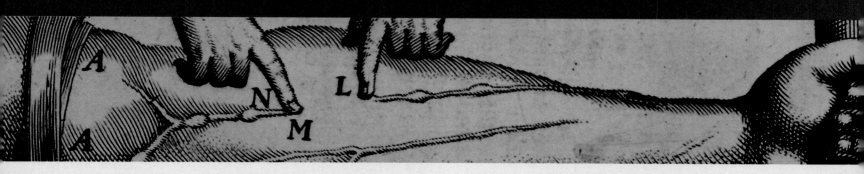

In turn, this enriched blood then traveled to the brain where it was infused with "animal spirit" and transported to all parts of the body through hollow nerve channels. If the humors were in balance, a person felt strong and well; if any part was out of harmony, sickness was the inevitable consequence. Galen also denied that the heart was a muscle on the ground that muscles, by definition, worked by voluntary action.

Over time, Galen's heirs simply hammered out the details of this humoral theory, going on to fit human physiology, pathology, and psychology within a grander philosophy of the entire harmonious universe. Remarkably, the system worked sufficiently well so that it was not seriously challenged until the 17th century. For nearly 1300 years, mainstream physicians healed by restoring the balance of humors within their patients, using heroic remedies to decrease some fluids and increase others. Consequently, they subjected their patients to sweating, emetics, laxatives, enemas, magical potions, and copious bloodletting. Of all these "therapeutics," no procedures proved more persistent or tenacious than the last, which enjoyed a degree of legitimacy until well into the 19th century. As if to bloodletting a scientific basis, medieval physicians—or more often barber-surgeons—took direction from one of the widely circulated "bleeding calendars." These were astronomical almanacs listing optimal days and body locations for the drawing of blood, all further broken down according to particular complaints and phases of the moon. In these centuries, whatever experience most students of medicine had with the actual workings of the body came principally from external observation. Although physicians of the Classical era had conducted systematic dissections of corpses to advance their understanding of human anatomy, this practice fell out of favor soon after Galen's death. Early Christians and, to a lesser extent, Jewish and Muslim theologians, regarded postmortem examinations as a sacrilege and banned the practice. Only when secular scientists and their royal allies gained sufficient ground to oppose papal edicts did anatomical studies resume, a change usually traced to The Holy Roman Emperor, Frederick II. This patron of the arts and sciences, founder of universities, and iconoclast issued a decree early in the 13th century requiring physicians trained at the Universities of Padua and Naples to attend an anatomy demonstration before graduating. The dissections were rather perfunctory, typically conducted by an assistant to the sound of the professor reading explanations from a Galenic text. Often the text was a sharp contradiction of the observable facts, though the students were usually too numerous and too far away for all but the most alert to note discrepancies anyway. Though anatomical texts and illustrations were produced, they tended to be idiosyncratic, grossly inaccurate, and in handwritten editions of one. (The first printed illustrated medical text appeared in 1491, nearly three decades after the first Gutenberg Bible, and it continued to reflect Galenic theory.) Consequently, the fragments of knowledge that were beginning to accumulate in a few centers of scientific investigation went largely unnoticed.

Andreas Vesalius, a Fleming who taught anatomy and surgery at the University of Padua, changed all that. In 1538, he published his abbreviated *Tabulae Anatomicae*, followed five years later by his more celebrated opus, *De Humani Corporis Fabrica*. *Tabulae* is a brief work containing just six annotated plates, two of which are devoted to the heart and circulatory system. *Fabrica* is a lengthy work of 85 plates including a dozen views of the heart, one in cross-section to show the relative thickness of the ventricular walls and the shape of its cavities. Considered a classic in both the science of medicine and the art of printing, *Fabrica* is astonishing both for its accuracy and for the beauty of its drawings, executed under his direction by Jan Stephen van Calcar, a student of Titian. Virtually every anatomy book that followed has used *Fabrica* as a model.

Vesalius' emphasis on nature as the best teacher influenced every other aspect of medical discovery to follow. In regard to developments in understanding the heart, the names of two 17th century scientists stand out: William Harvey and Marcello Malpighi. Englishman William Harvey went to Padua to study under Fabricius, whose own teacher had been one of Vesalius' students. And it was Harvey, his curiosity piqued by Fabricius' demonstration of valves in the veins, who in 1628 revealed another major medical truth— blood moves through the body within a closed circulating system. This discovery, which contradicted traditional doctrine, completed the assault on Galenic authority so magnificently begun by Vesalian anatomy.

Malpighi, an Italian physician and anatomist by profession, was one of the early microscopists, perhaps the first whose frame of reference was specifically medical. Malpighi succeeded in supplying the answer to the one problem Harvey could only guess at: how blood flowing outward from the heart through the arteries is able to return by means of the veins. The capillaries which Harvey could not see, Malpighi found. He wrote about them in *De Pulmonis Observationis*, 1661. With this mystery finally solved, modern medicine could begin to take shape.

JUSTI CORTNUMMII
DE
MORBO ATTONITO
LIBER UNUS
Cum Gratia et Privilegio Sacrae Caesareae Majest: et Elect: Saxon.

GALENUS   Scilicet hic spinas colligit: ille rosas.   HIPPOCRATES
LIPSIÆ
SUMPTIBUS GEORGII HEINRICI FROMMANNI.

Hippocrates (c. 460-379 BC) gave Greek medicine its scientific spirit as well as its storied ethical ideals. According to Hippocratic theory, all disease stemmed from disorders or imbalances of the body fluids. These teachings spread throughout the Mediterranean world and beyond, through the influence of the great Greek physician-scientist Galen (130-200 AD) to remain the dominant belief until the late 16th century. The illustration above, depicting Hippocrates (right) and Galen (left), is taken from a 17th century medical text. The artist uses the opportunity to deliver some not-so-subtle personal commentary on the influences of these two men: where Hippocrates touches the bush between them, it flowers; under Galen's influence, it produces nothing but thorns.

Theriac was a medicinal preparation devised as a universal antidote to virtually anything that ailed a patient, heart palpitations included. Theriac's origins are thought to date back to the time of Mithridates, King of Pontus (120-63 BC), who achieved a reputation in the art of giving and taking poisons, a form of experimental pharmacology. Galen, who used medications on a far grander scale, further elaborated theriac, making it a virtual witches' brew of some 70 ingredients. By the Renaissance, the number of parts in a theriac recipe might exceed 100, with preparation of the cure-all being an annual ritual in some communities. Here, in a pharmaceutical guidebook printed in Stuttgart, Germany, in 1537, two apothecaries are shown mixing the latest batch that will then be aged, much like wine, for maximum potency.

Until little more than a century ago, the vascular surgeon was limited to treating only minor arterial aneurysms and these with the simplest of tools. Primitive peoples used stone knives made of obsidian, sharpening them by fracturing an edge or by heating them in the fire. In the Ebers Papyrus, c. 2000 BC, we read that when encountering "a tumor of the vessels in any part of the body…and thou findest it round in form, growing under thy finger…[the physician should] treat it with the knife and burn it with the fire so that it bleeds not too much." By the time of Hippocrates, if not before, control of hemorrhage through pressure and ligature was also understood. Celsus, who lived c. 40 AD, added that when profuse bleeding proved difficult to stop, "the veins that are pouring out blood are to be seized…and tied in two places, and cut across in between, so that each end may retract on itself and yet have its orifice closed." By the 11th century, when this illustration from an Anglo-Saxon manuscript appeared, cautery for the destruction of tissue and the closing of veins and arteries was widely practiced. Albucasis, an Arabic physician of Moorish, Spain and unique among his peers for his interest in surgery, wrote a book devoted to the subject of cautery about this time. Albucasis recommended cautery as having "universal application for every ill constitution, whether organic or functional."

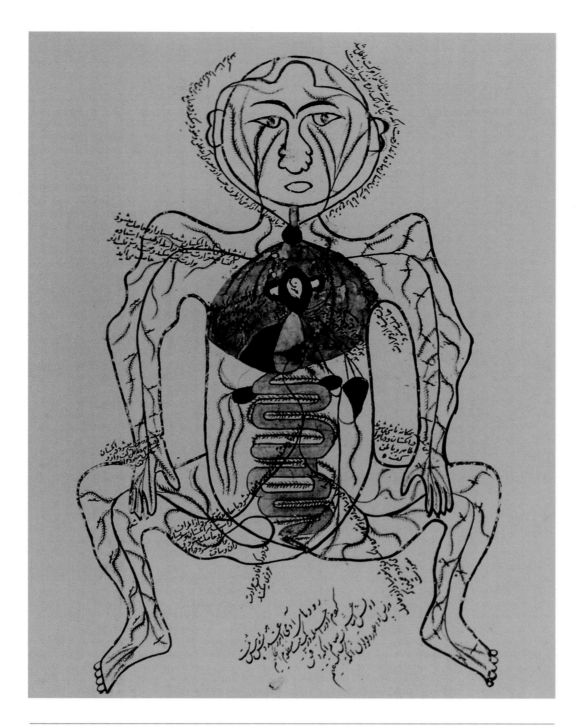

During the Middle Ages, Arabic medicine was the dominant school of therapeutics throughout the Mediterranean world. Arabic physicians used essentially the same methods as the Western followers of Galen, though with certain important differences. Religious beliefs caused Arabic healers to downgrade the role of surgical intervention, with the result that surgeons and physicians became truly separate divisions within medical practice for many centuries thereafter. Many aspects of cutting, cauterizing, bandaging, bleeding, and cupping were left to untrained folk doctors and others without formalized training. At the same time, Arabic practitioners elevated the importance of botanical medicines, contributing significantly to the development of pharmacology and chemistry as separate major disciplines. Their greatest theoretician was Avicenna, a Persian, whose 11th century Canon of Medicine probably provided the information on which this anatomical drawing of the body and its circulatory system was based. It comes from the Treatise of Anatomy by Mansur ibn Muhammad, who flourished c. 1400. Incidentally, the author listed 63 cardiac drugs in his text. Like most Arabic physicians of his time, Mansur also believed the heart to have only three chambers.

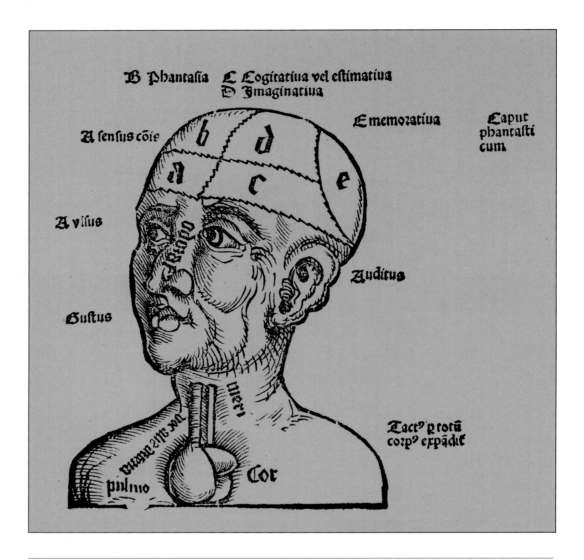

Because physicians and surgeons continued to be less than fully informed about the internal structure of the body, anatomical drawings remained somewhat speculative until well into the Renaissance. Here, in a 1513 medical text by Frenchman Matthias Qualle of Haguenau, the heart is shown as an undersized organ whose location would seem to be more closely related to that of the "Adam's Apple" than to its actual position in the chest cavity.

By the 17th century, a skilled physician/surgeon might have a number of cautery tools in his kit. Shown here are assorted instruments as delineated in the Armamentarium Chirurgicum Bipartitum, *written by the German physician Joannis Gerlini, Frankfurt, 1666. About this time, the notion of ligating arteries began to return to favor as an alternative method. Neither system was very successful in stemming significant bleeding or preventing infection. One example of the more usual outcome of treating arterial wounds comes from Peter Lowe, a 16th century Scottish surgeon. Describing a cautery procedure he had seen in France involving a wounded soldier suffering from aneurysm, Lowe tells of a barber-surgeon who "without further ado, opened the swelling with a lancet, and blood spewed out so violently that the captain died some hours later. I do not doubt that many such mistakes of the art are committed by the fools in these countries."*

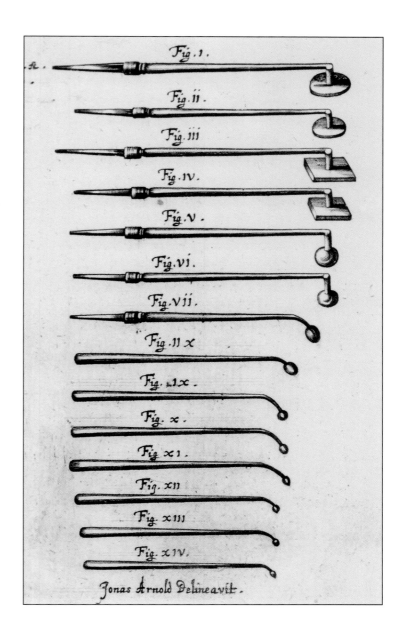

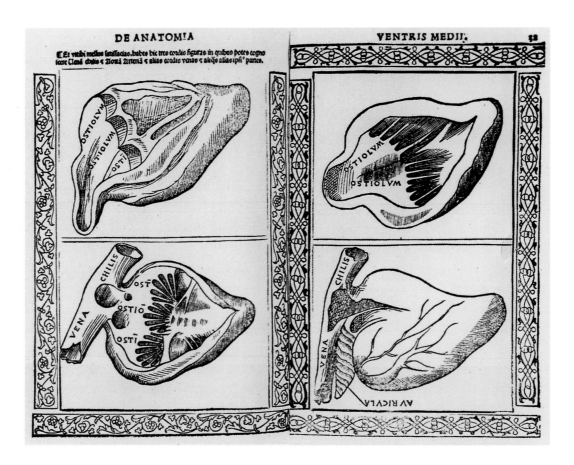

Above: The first anatomical illustrations made consistently from nature were produced by Jacopo Berengario da Carpi, a Bolognese anatomist and contemporary of Vesalius. These four views of the heart in various stages of dissection appeared in Berengario's Isagogae, a short anatomical supplement to his 1521 Commentaria. As most anatomists of this period restricted themselves to drawing skeletons and muscles, these images of viscera are doubly unusual. Berengario claimed to have dissected several hundred bodies during his career, and he certainly displayed more detailed knowledge of the body than any of his predecessors.

Right: As the papacy gradually reduced its sanctions against surgical dissections and autopsies of cadavers, the ability of physicians to understand the structure of the human body and its organs progressed slowly. The illustration is from Spiegel der Artzny, 1518, by the Dutch physician and geographer Laurentius Frisius. Though relatively crude and faulted in its depiction of the skeleton, it is nonetheless unusual for its time in the extent to which it depicts the viscera. Following a format frequently followed in medieval bleeding almanacs—a central figure surrounded by a series of smaller images—it also includes six insets depicting the anatomy of the brain and a tongue. They are realistic enough to appear to be based on an actual dissection.

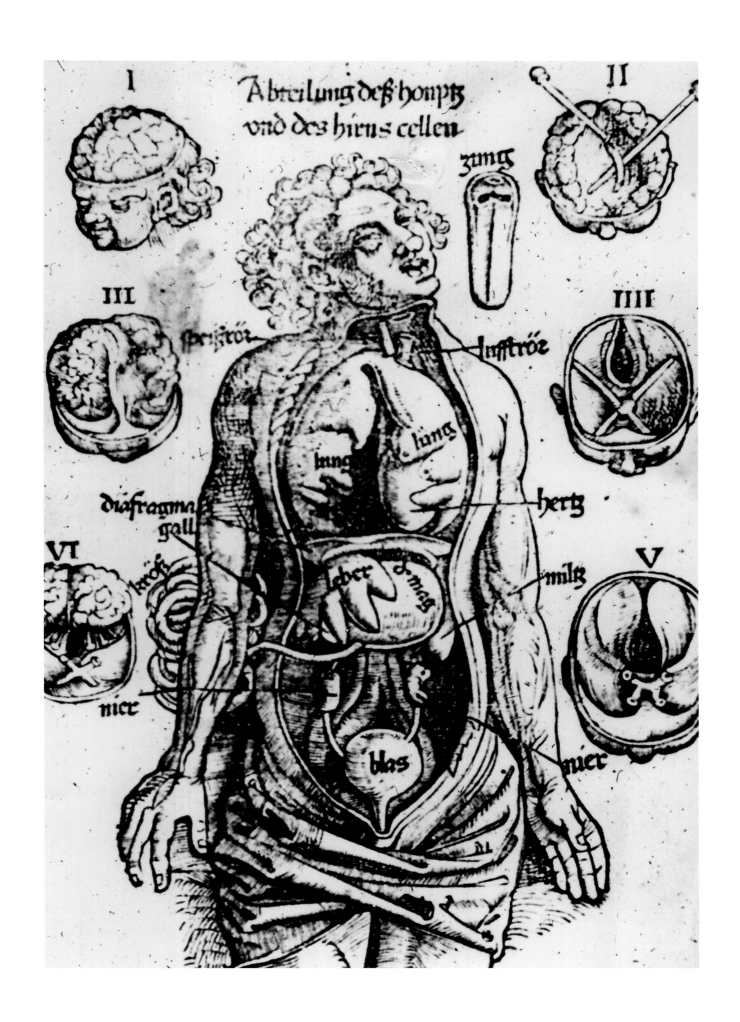

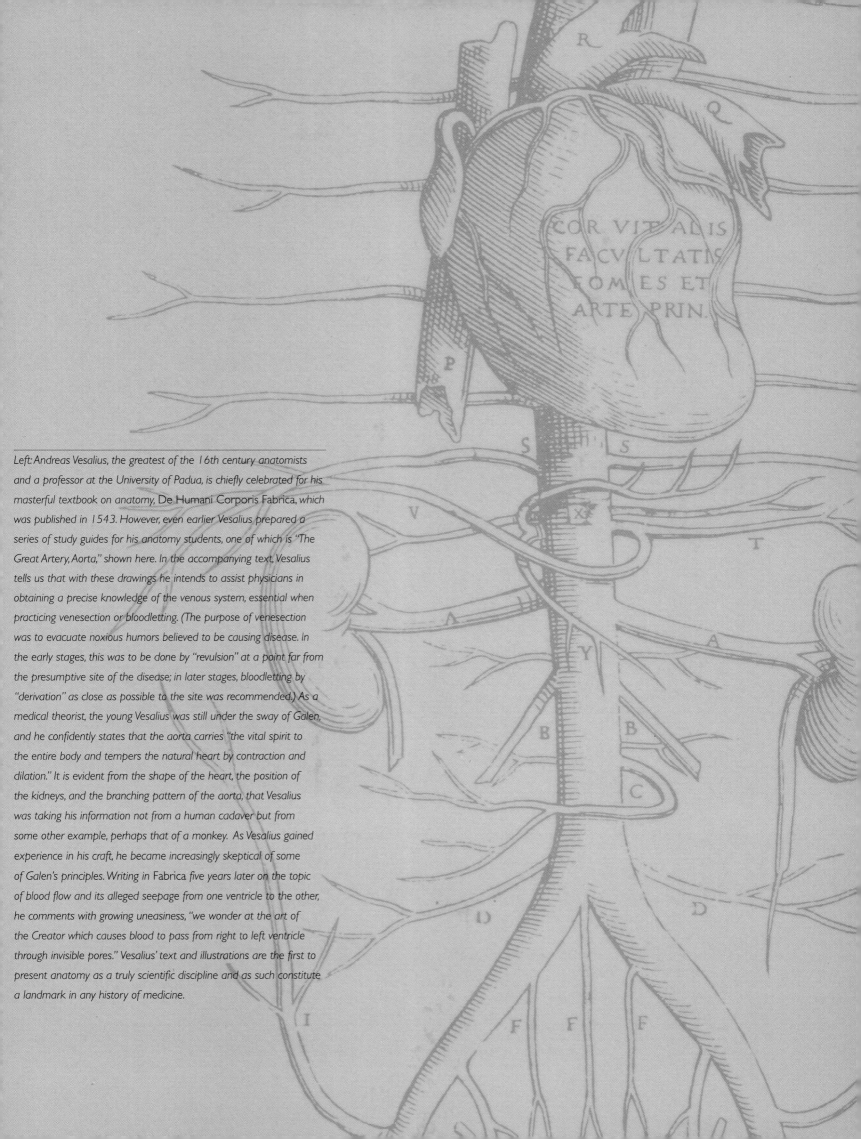

Left: Andreas Vesalius, the greatest of the 16th century anatomists and a professor at the University of Padua, is chiefly celebrated for his masterful textbook on anatomy, De Humani Corporis Fabrica, which was published in 1543. However, even earlier Vesalius prepared a series of study guides for his anatomy students, one of which is "The Great Artery, Aorta," shown here. In the accompanying text, Vesalius tells us that with these drawings he intends to assist physicians in obtaining a precise knowledge of the venous system, essential when practicing venesection or bloodletting. (The purpose of venesection was to evacuate noxious humors believed to be causing disease. In the early stages, this was to be done by "revulsion" at a point far from the presumptive site of the disease; in later stages, bloodletting by "derivation" as close as possible to the site was recommended.) As a medical theorist, the young Vesalius was still under the sway of Galen, and he confidently states that the aorta carries "the vital spirit to the entire body and tempers the natural heart by contraction and dilation." It is evident from the shape of the heart, the position of the kidneys, and the branching pattern of the aorta, that Vesalius was taking his information not from a human cadaver but from some other example, perhaps that of a monkey. As Vesalius gained experience in his craft, he became increasingly skeptical of some of Galen's principles. Writing in Fabrica five years later on the topic of blood flow and its alleged seepage from one ventricle to the other, he comments with growing uneasiness, "we wonder at the art of the Creator which causes blood to pass from right to left ventricle through invisible pores." Vesalius' text and illustrations are the first to present anatomy as a truly scientific discipline and as such constitute a landmark in any history of medicine.

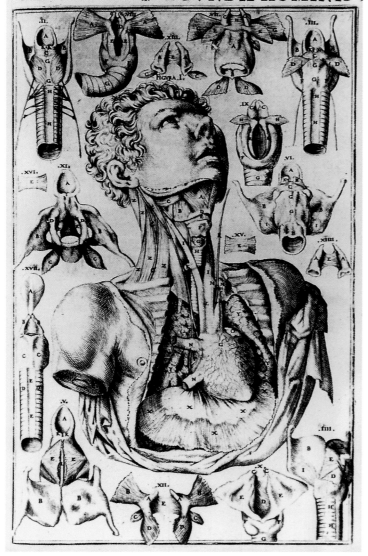

By the end of the 16th century, Vesalian anatomy had become a mainstay of surgical practice in western Europe and many fine details were beginning to be added to the picture as well. In 1603, Hieronymus Fabricius, one of the giants of medical teaching at that time, published a study of the veins that contained the first accurate descriptions and illustrations of the venous valves. Another important contributor to the Italian anatomical tradition was Giulio Casserio. His Tabulae Anatomicae, from which these two illustrations are taken, was published in 1601.

Towering above all other achievements in medicine in the 17th century was that of English physician William Harvey, a contemporary of William Shakespeare. Harvey, shown above, obtained his early medical training in England. He later went abroad to the Italian city of Padua to study medicine in greater detail. There, he was fortunate to become the pupil of Fabricius, and through Fabricius a direct intellectual descendant of Vesalius. Returning to England, Harvey was soon appointed court physician, first to James I and later to Charles I.

In this contemporary painting by Robert Hannah, Harvey is shown demonstrating his experiments on deer hearts to his patron, King Charles, and courtiers. Harvey's sinecure ended with the Puritans' overthrow of the throne and Charles' beheading in 1649, but Harvey was still able to continue his research, carrying out hundreds of clever and ingenious experiments in blood circulation before his own natural death in 1657 at the advanced age of 79.

EXERCITATIO

ANATOMICA DE
MOTV CORDIS ET SAN-
GVINIS IN ANIMALI-
BVS,

GVILIELMI HARVEI ANGLI,
Medici Regii, & Professoris Anatomiæ in Col-
legio Medicorum Londinensi.

FRANCOFVRTI,
Sumptibus GVILIELMI FITZERI.

ANNO M. DC. XXVIII.

Harvey's assault on Galenic theory climaxed with the publication in 1628 of his Excitatio Anatomica
de Motu Cordis, *or* On the Motion of the Heart and Blood. *The result of careful observation and
experimentation, this work provided the first reasoned proof that blood flowed from the heart in a
continuous one-way cycle. Further, he found that the heart acts in an essentially mechanical fashion;
its muscular chambers force-pump the blood outward to parts of the body through a system of
arteries and bring back the same blood through a complementary system of veins. Though Harvey
lacked a microscope and could not see the intervening capillaries, he reasoned correctly that something
like them must exist.*

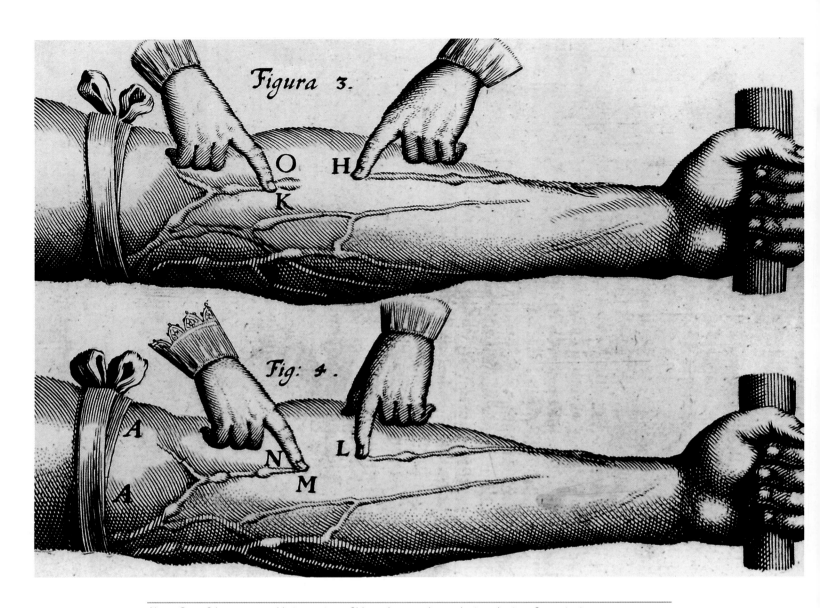

---

*Above: One of the many notable innovations of Harvey's research was the introduction of quantitative measurement.
Harvey began with the information, based on studies of cadavers, that the heart holds only two ounces of blood;
and since it beats on average 72 times per minute, he further calculated that in a full hour this same muscle would
pump 8640 ounces into the circulatory system, roughly three times the weight of an average man. From this, he
concluded that there was no possible way the body could produce or rid itself of so much blood on the basis of daily
food intake. Only a closed, one-way system would be practicable. The illustration above, from De motu cordis, shows
one of Harvey's experiments in which he "milks the vein downward" to demonstrate the one-way action of the valves.*

---

*Right: Oxford-trained Robert Fludd of England was both physician and mystic philosopher. As a philosopher, he sought
a unity between the macrocosmic universe and the microcosmic world of individual humans. Following this reasoning,
he concluded that the heart was the center of the body in the same way that the sun was the center of the solar
system. He illustrated this principle on the title page of his Medicine Catholica, published in 1629. It shows in
allegorical form the hand of God taking the pulse of man above a circle cluttered with skulls and bones and
depictions of the earth's four winds. The quotation inscribed in the circle is from Ezekiel 37, "Behold, I will cause
breath to enter into you, and ye shall live." Fludd was notable for being among the very first medical men of stature
to come to the support of William Harvey's heretical views of blood circulation.*

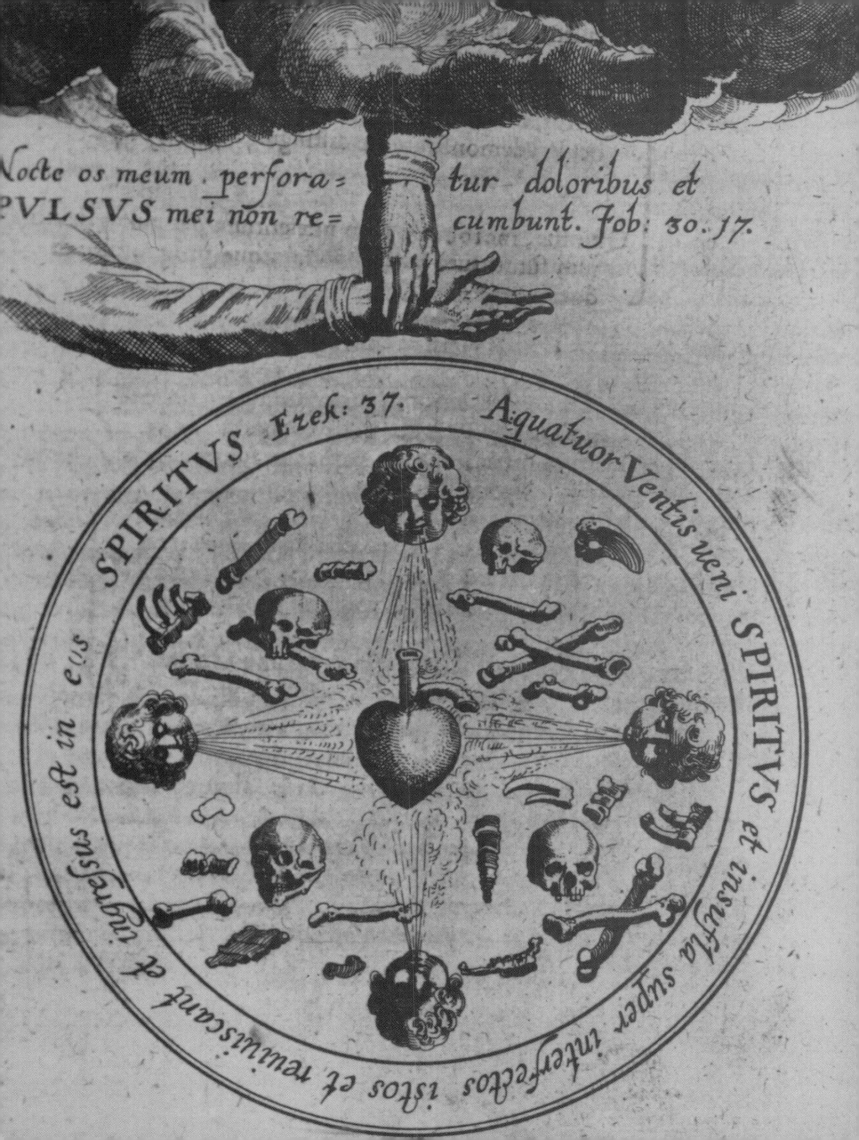

Nocte os meum perfora= tur doloribus et
PVLSVS mei non re= cumbunt. Job: 30. 17.

SPIRITVS Ezek: 37. A quatuor Ventis veni SPIRITVS et insufla super interfectos istos et reuiuscant et ingressus est in eis

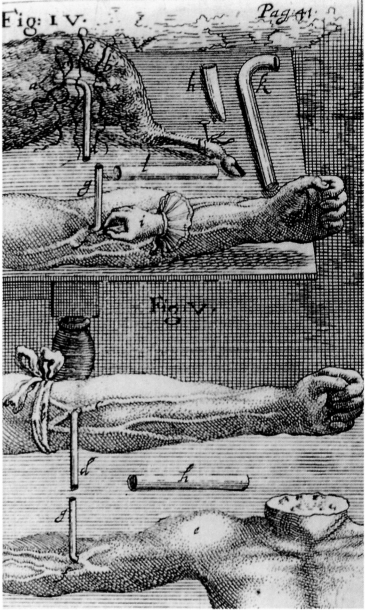

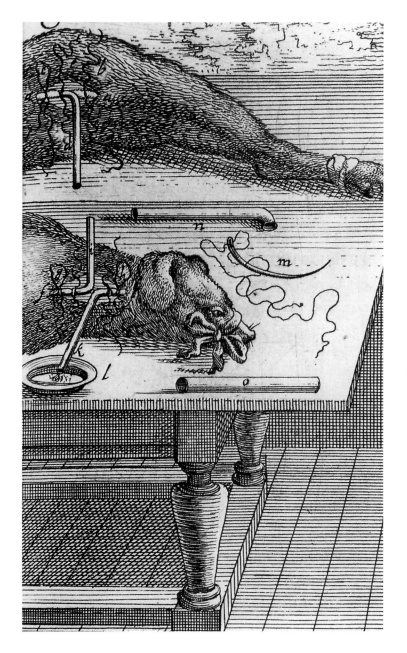

The idea of transfusing blood from a healthy person to a sick one is very ancient. Ancient peoples drank the blood of their enemies for strength. Some speculate that a similar notion was behind the reported deathbed attempt of Pope Innocent VII to restore his health, when he is said to have drunk the blood taken from three ten-year-old boys in 1492. All of the participants in the papal "cure" reportedly died. Interest in transfusion was renewed following Harvey's work on circulation, and in the latter half of the 17th century repeated experiments are recorded. One German physician who took the time to write about it was Johann Elsholtz, whose 1665 Clysmatic Nova contains a series of illustrations showing how blood might be transfused into an arm or leg vein via a simple hypodermic device. A small knife, a tourniquet for raising the vein, and a vial possibly containing a substance to cleanse the skin, are also part of the equipment recommended. As the risks of using unmatched blood types was as yet unknown, the first authenticated transfusions were performed from animals, typically sheep, to humans. Richard Lower of England and Jean-Baptiste Denis, physician to Louis XIV, both achieved human to human transfusions in 1667. But misuse of the technique—Denis attempted to dampen the sexual appetites of an overzealous young man by transfusing him with the blood of a mild-mannered calf leading to the young man's death—prompted the authorities to ban the practice altogether. Few if any transfusions were given for the next 150 years.

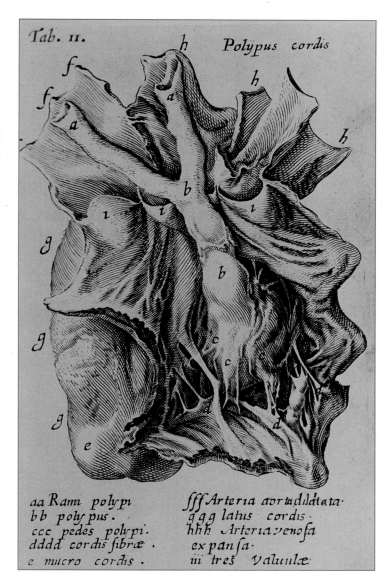

Above: Dr. Tulp, who was a practicing physician and member of the Surgeons' Guild of Amsterdam, published Medical Observations, *a detailed medical treatise, in 1641. Included in his text was this engraving showing a polyp of the heart. Tulp is better remembered today for his pioneering descriptions of the deficiency disease, beriberi, and his description of the ileocecal or Tulp's valve.*

Left: Once dissection was made legal, the teaching of anatomy using cadavers came out of the shadows. The Dutch, in particular, celebrated this change, making anatomy lessons not only a key facet of medical education but a form of entertainment for curious citizens who were also permitted to attend. The first anatomical theater was built around this time in Leyden, and painters, recognizing the public's fascination with what went on there, recorded many such gatherings on canvas. Here, in a portrait by Rembrandt finished in 1632, the much-admired Dr. Nicolaus Tulp is seen in the midst of a lecture before a group of unidentified gentlemen. Dr. Tulp is demonstrating the workings of nerves in the arm, and Rembrandt was accurate enough to show the cadaver's hand in splayed position, just as it would appear in real life.

L'HOMME

DE RENE'

DESCARTES.

ET VN TRAITTÉ

DE LA FORMATION DV FOETVS

DV MESME AVTHEVR.

Auec les Remarques de LOVYS DE LA FORGE,
Docteur en Medecine, demeurant à la Fleche,
Sur le Traitté de l'Homme de RENE' DESCARTES;
& sur les Figures par luy inuentées.

A PARIS,

Chez CHARLES ANGOT, Libraire Iuré, ruë
S. Iacques, au Lion d'Or.

M. DC. LXIV.

AVEC PRIVILEGE DV ROY.

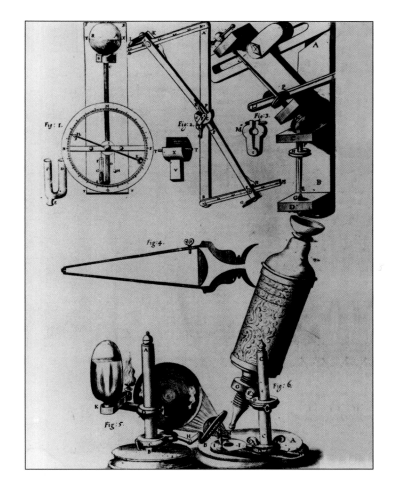

A critical early step toward expanding medical understanding in the 17th century was the development of the microscope. The magnifying glass had been known since at least the 13th century, but it took centuries more to devise a means to put it to practical use. Dutchman Antonie van Leeuwenhoek, a draper and watchman of Delft, as well as an amateur scientist of remarkable gifts, is generally credited with devising the first simple micro-scopes in the last third of the 17th century. But high magnification was possible only with the development of a compound microscope, containing at least two lenses. This improvement was achieved in 1662 by Englishman Robert Hooke. The illustration (left), from Hooke's Micrographia, published in 1665, shows his remarkable micro-scope, a lens grinding machine (upper right) and various other inventions.

Left: Seventeenth century western medicine is sometimes described as falling into two camps—iatrophysics and iatrochemistry. Iatrophysics regarded the body as analogous to a machine operating under the laws of mathematics and physics. Iatrochemistry perceived the body as governed by a series of processes that were entirely chemical in nature. In this philosophical split, the Frenchman René Descartes was distinctly an iatrophysicist. Writing in his Treatise of Man, 1664, whose title page is shown here, Descartes declared that cardiac heat, which he termed "fire without light," was generated by the agitation of blood particles. He equated the warmth of the heart, not the soul, with life itself. Descartes further believed that the beating heart fills with blood by means of gravity, the drops of blood dripping into the cavities from the veins, and that the heart empties through fermentation. As the blood vaporizes, the heart dilates, opening its valves to permit the escape of blood. Though Cartesian theory represented some dramatic advances over earlier knowledge, Descartes' ideas on the heart and circulation were largely in conflict with Harvey's discoveries and ultimately proved misguided.

Above: Capillaries, which had been hinted at by William Harvey, were first identified by Marcello Malpighi, professor of anatomy at Bologna and Pisa, papal physician, and trained microscopist. Malpighi's discoveries were widely disseminated even during his lifetime, because he had the vision to join scientific organizations such as Britain's Royal Society. Through them he was able to share his ideas in the form of papers submitted to the Society's Transactions.

Right: In writing about his discoveries, Malpighi credited the lowly frog as his collaborator, for it was thanks to the wonderful transparency of the frogs' lungs that the microscopist was able to see the fine structures with such remarkable clarity. In the same way, he could see that the blood in their capillaries flowed only in the direction of the veins. Shown here is an illustration of the pulmonary circulation of a frog, with a cross-sectional microscopic view showing its vascular structures. The image appeared in Opera Omnia, *1687, one of the several texts written by Malpighi that have earned him the rank of founder of histology and biologic microscopy. In another work, Malpighi also characterized red blood corpuscles, describing them as "fat globules looking like a rosary of red coral."*

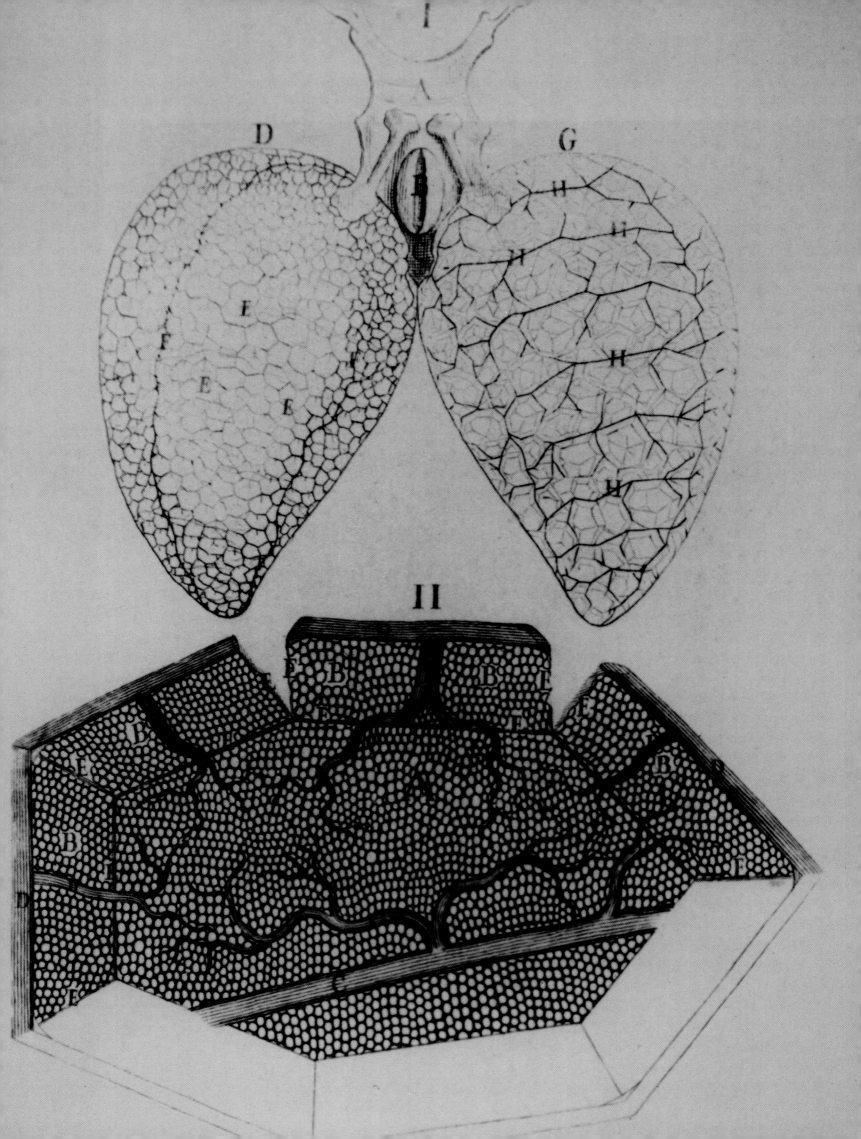

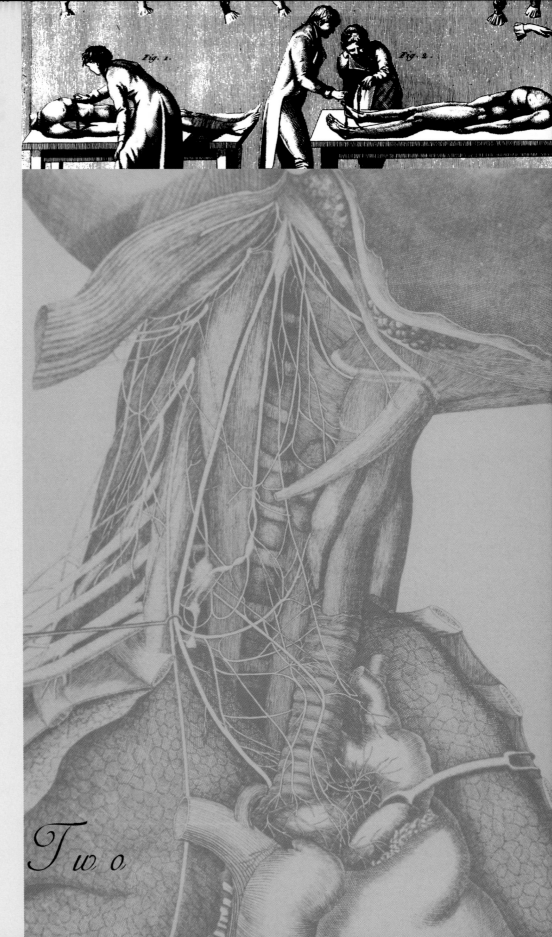

Chapter Two

THE HEART HAS ITS REASONS

The 18th century is known as the Age of Enlightenment, a time when rationalism, classification, order, and empiricism were the organizing principles of science as well as social and political thought in the West. Just as physician and botanist Carl von Linné devised his *Systema naturae* in 1735 as a means of categorizing all living things, so 18th century Europeans engaged in other aspects of medicine tended toward the systematic ordering of knowledge. Specialized textbooks on facets of internal medicine, monographs on the uses of various drugs, and accurate descriptions of many diseases based on their symptoms and pathology, all made their first appearances in this era. So too, electricity's effects on the heart were first noted with amazement. As news and knowledge still traveled slowly, Americans remained at the distant end of most advances and contributed little on their own.

Concerning the heart in particular, notable British additions to the literature include William Cowper's work on aortic insufficiency in 1706; Stephen Hales' investigation of blood pressure, published in 1733; William Hunter's description of arteriovenous aneurysms in 1757; William Heberden's monograph on angina pectoris in 1768; and William Withering's treatise on digitalis in 1785. France added the discoveries of Raymond Vieussens, a professor at Montpellier, who made numerous observations useful in diagnosing pathologies of the heart, including aortic insufficiency, pericardial adhesions, and the relationship of heart disease to pulmonary disease.

Italy had an outstanding systematizer in Giovanni Battista Morgagni, whose *De Sedibus et Causis Morborum,* 1761, gave the first recorded descriptions of diseases of the cardiac valves and of mitral stenosis and heart-block (Stokes-Adams disease). Morgagni did not explore in any depth the concept of how heart diseases might develop, nor did he directly correlate the pathology of coronary vessels and heart disease, but he stands out as the first major figure to present a detailed catalog of disease pathology in general. Equally important, Morgagni based his findings on direct evidence gathered during hundreds of autopsies. And finally, Switzerland's Albrecht von Haller wrote the first comprehensive treatises on physiology between 1752 and 1766. In the process, he provided an informed explanation for why and how the heart pulsated. He also compiled the first critical bibliography of anatomy, medicine, and surgery, evaluating the works of more than 5,000 authors from the days of medieval manuscripts to his own time.

Anatomic treatises and atlases continued to break new ground during the century, and while the Italians remained preeminent, centers of reputable anatomic work appeared in many other parts of Europe as well. A number of starts were made in introducing quantitative measurements to medical diagnosis: in 1710 John Floyer devised a wristwatch to measure the human pulse; in 1740 George Martine introduced the concept of clinical thermometry as a diagnostic tool; and in 1751 Leopold Auenbrugger wrote a short book describing how a physician might percuss a patient's chest to learn useful information regarding various disease states. Unfortunately, its value would not be widely appreciated for another half century.

Progress was made in the art and technique of surgery, too, though rarely of the caliber occurring in internal medicine. The majority of men drawn to practice surgery still tended to be less educated, less prone to observation, and more likely to pride themselves on their speed and daring than on their scientific rationale. And centuries of abuses and indiscretions by some of their unskilled barber-surgeon ancestors made the respectability enjoyed by physicians still somewhat elusive. Most surgeons continued to specialize in bleeding and amputation, with occasional forays into setting bones. (Incidentally, British surgeons of this era still identified their premises by the striped barber pole, the pole representing the staff gripped by patients to promote bleeding, with the red and white stripes emblematic of the blood and the tourniquet.) Three surgeons who did attain a deserved reputation for innovative work, particularly in regard to the heart and circulation, were Richard Lambert, as well as John and William Hunter.

Lambert, a surgeon at England's Newcastle Infirmary, appears to have carried out the first successful arterial repair by means of suturing. Lambert, in describing his innovation, said he had come to believe that suturing was a safe alternative to amputation in some cases of arterial wounds. He based this on his observation of the way other kinds of wounds healed naturally. When a patient presented with a bleeding aneurysm in the summer of 1759, he decided to give it a try. Writes Lambert, "The artery was laid bare and its wound discovered; and the tourniquet being now slackened, the gush of blood per saltum showed there was no deception. Next, two ligatures, one above the orifice and one below, were passed under the artery, that they might be ready to be tied at any time, in case the method proposed should fail. Then a small steel pin, rather more than a quarter inch long, was passed through the two lips of the wound in the artery, and secured by twisting a thread around it, as in the harelip. This was found to stop the bleeding; upon which the wound was bound up." Lambert concluded his report by saying that the patient was put to bed, the wound dressed occasionally, and in due course the pins and the ligatures removed as the blood was observed to course fully through the repaired vessel. Lambert thought the technique might well prevent the loss of many arms and legs in the future.

John Hunter's contribution to coronary surgery began with his investigations of the horn-shedding of deer. He reasoned that just as the supply of blood to the base of the horns changes according to the activity needed to grow and shed them, so the human vascular system is sufficiently dynamic that it can sometimes grow or expand secondary vessels to maintain blood flow around occluded arteries. This premise provided the framework for treating arterial aneurysms with ligation. An opportunity presented itself in 1775 when a coachman complaining of a 3-year-long painful and pulsating aneurysm in his knee-fold appeared at St. George's Hospital. Hunter thought that because the condition had existed so long without causing gangrene, this indicated that a reasonable blood supply to the lower extremity still existed. He decided to try removing the aneurysm and save the leg. Cutting into a place henceforth known as Hunter's channel—along the inner thigh just above the knee—he tied under the large thigh artery at four points, to avoid great pressure at any one location. He then drained the aneurysm, closed up, and waited for the wound to heal, which it did with only brief septic reverses. In subsequent months, he repeated the operation on four other patients, three of which ended successfully, a remarkable surgical achievement at a time when neither anesthesia nor antisepsis was available.

Blood transfusions, though officially outlawed in many countries, were once again tried occasionally as last-ditch treatments. Witness the description written by Erasmus Darwin, grandfather of Charles Darwin, of a procedure he recommended to one of his elderly patients. Hoping to supply him with a few ounces of young blood daily, he proposed first "to fix a silver pipe about an inch long to each extremity of a chicken's gut;...to put one end into the vein of a person hired for that purpose, so as to receive the blood returning from the extremity; and when the gut was quite full, and the blood running through the other silver end, to introduce that end into the vein of the patient upwards toward the heart, so as to admit no air along with the blood." Darwin's patient took 24 hours to think about it and then told the doctor that he would prefer to let nature take its course, which it did a few days later.

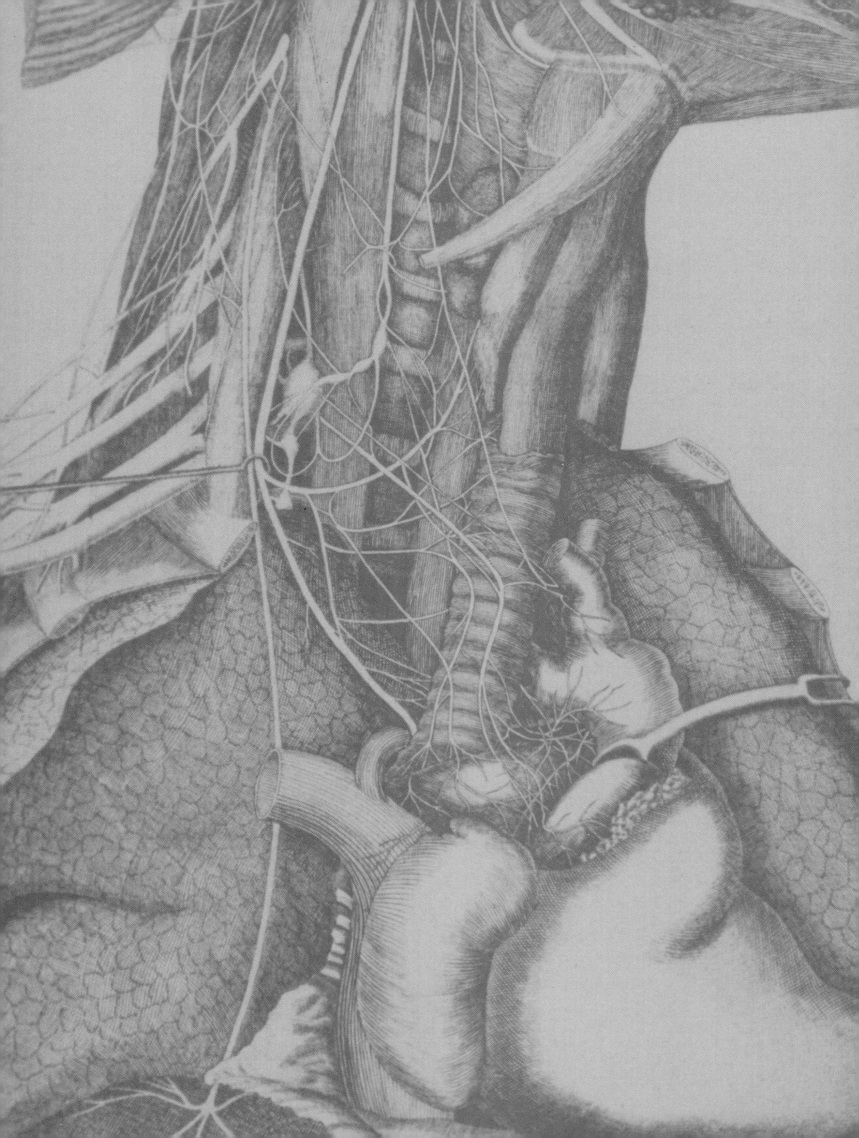

Left: With Vesalius' anatomical drawings as the model, the Italian schools of anatomy continued to maintain their traditional leadership in this adjunct of medical investigation. But now there were other European countries where careful, reputable work was also being done, often with the added benefit of copper engravings to record them. One of the little known, but accomplished, anatomical surgeons working in Germany in the 18th century was Johann Ernst Neubauer of Frankfurt. This illustration appeared in his Descriptio Anatomica Nervorum Cardiacorum, *a text published in 1772.*

Above: An eminent anatomist, physiologist, and botanist, as well as poet, philosopher, and master bibliographer, Albrecht von Haller has been described as a universal genius. During his career at the University of Göttingen, Hanover, which he helped to found in 1737, he wrote some 13,000 scientific papers. von Haller then retired to his native Bern, Switzerland, to carry out extensive research. In 1752 he published On the Irritable and Sensible Parts of the Body, *in which he developed the idea that certain parts of the body possessed "sensibility" and reacted to pain, while others operated according to "irritability" and reacted by contracting when stimulated. This led von Haller to postulate that the heart, as the most irritable organ in the body, with many layers of muscular fibers capable of reacting, pulsed when the inflow of blood caused it to contract in response to irritation. The illustration above appeared in von Haller's other major work,* Physiological Elements of the Human Body, *that was published in its entirety in 1766. The illustration depicts the body of a small dog about to be dissected. Cherubs stand beside a large heart and hold up an anatomical chart for admiration. This text has been called the first comprehensive treatise on physiology, placing von Haller among the giants of medical progress.*

In Haemastatics, which the Rev. Hales published in 1733, medicine had its first quantitative study of blood pressure. Hales began his investigations in an effort to settle the controversial question whether blood pressure was in any way related to muscular motion. As he described, "It occurred to me that by fixing tubes to the arteries of live animals, I might find pretty nearly whether the blood, by its mere hydraulic energy, could have a sufficient force, by dilating the fibers of the acting muscles and thereby shortening their lengths, to produce the great effects of muscular motion." Hales tied down a live mare, inserted a hollow tube into its neck artery, attached and suspended a glass column to the tube, and saw the blood rise nine feet in the column. Hales also noted that the blood did not rise to its full height at once; rather, it went half way at once and then gradually rose at each pulse. Hales went on to make comparative studies of dogs, sheep, oxen, and humans, carefully calculating their respective weight, tubular height to which their blood ascended, cubic capacity of their respective hearts, pulse rate, velocity of flow, and so on. Hales also examined the factors that he believed were instrumental in maintaining blood pressure, including cardiac output and the resistance of peripheral vessels. Noting that the resistance was variable according to perfusions added to the blood flow, he theorized that vasodilation and vasoconstriction were associated phenomena. He also concluded that blood pressure was not, after all, directly related to muscular motion.

Right: Stephen Hales, a Cambridge-trained clergyman with no formal training in science or medicine, was blessed with the sort of wonderful curiosity about the natural world that distinguished so many 18th century gentlemen. Throughout a lifetime of service as curate in the English village of Teddington, Hales pursued an active interest in the hydraulics of living organisms, both plant and animal. In his 1727 Vegetable Staticks, *from which this title page is taken, he measured rates of plant growth, suction force of roots, and sap pressure in the branching plant. His innovative work in plant physiology was a prelude to his still more significant work in blood pressure.*

THE REVᴰ Dᴿ STEPHEN HALES, F.R.S.
AUTHOR OF VEGETABLE STATICS

The first authority to describe angina pectoris in detail was clinician William Heberden, who lectured in 1768 at the British Royal College of Surgeons on "A Disorder of the Breast." Heberden told his peers that "there is one ailment in the chest which has difficult and peculiar symptoms. It should be heeded, as it is neither free of danger nor particularly uncommon...Its localization, the patient's feeling of suffocation, and anguish accompanying it, give reason for calling it angina pectoris." Heberden went on to say that "those who are affected with it are seized while they are walking [more especially if it be uphill and soon after eating] with a painful and most disagreeable sensation in the breast that seems as if it could extinguish life if it were to increase or continue; but the moment they stand still all this uneasiness vanishes." Heberden was a scrupulous observer and his Commentaries, published in 1802, contains a lifetime of careful note-taking on scores of other diseases as well.

William Cullen, seen at an advanced age, was Scotland's most celebrated and inspiring medical teacher in the 18th century. Students came from all over the British Isles to hear him, in part because he spoke on medical topics in vernacular English in an era when Latin was the conventional language of science. The basis of Cullen's teaching was that life is a function of nervous energy, that muscle is a continuation of nerve, and that disease is mostly a result of breakdowns in nerve-to-muscle communication, or neuropathology. His ideas were more speculative than scientific, but because of his wide-ranging influence, they served to stimulate discussion and thus benefited theoretical science in his day. In 1757 Cullen published A History of Aneurisms of the Aorta.

Brothers William and John Hunter were Britain's best-known surgeons in the 18th century. William's anatomical school on Great Windmill Street, London, attracted scores of students from England, the Continent, and occasionally the British Colonies. So great was his school's need for cadavers as learning tools that the means of acquiring them became suspect, and he was charged with body-snatching. In this satirical drawing printed in 1773, the spindly-legged surgeon is shown scurrying off as his accomplice is caught red-handed, the corpus delicti spilling out of its basket in the process. William's contribution to the growth of a knowledge of the heart and circulatory system was his 1757 description of arteriovenous aneurysms and fistulae. Within two years of its publication, one of his protégés, Richard Lambert, performed the first recorded suture of a damaged artery. John Hunter, the greater technician of the two brothers, raised surgery from a mechanical craft to a science grounded in physiology and pathology. Probably his greatest contribution was the discovery that collateral arterial pathways will develop around damaged arteries following ligation. This led to a new technique—ligation of aneurysms—an alternative to amputation, previously the only means of dealing with many conditions. Hunter, who personally suffered from several ills, was especially troubled with angina, which he noted could be triggered by stress. "My life lies in the hands of whoever irritates me," he once commented. As predicted, he died of a heart attack suffered during a particularly contentious meeting with hospital staff.

Digitalis purpurea

William Withering, a physician by training but a botanist by avocation, is remembered for his discovery of the medical use of digitalis, a natural diuretic extracted from the dried and powdered leaf of the purple foxglove plant. In Withering's 1785 Account of the Foxglove, in which this botanical illustration appeared, he states that "It has a power over the motion of the heart to a degree yet unobserved in any other medicine." Withering was drawn to his experiments after learning of a folk cure used by an old Shropshire woman for the dropsy accompanying heart failure. The home remedy, Withering said, was composed of some 20 herbs, but he deduced that the active ingredient in countering dropsy was foxglove, which he knew to be a diuretic. Withering first experimented with digitalis among his charity patients—why risk his reputation on his paying customers—and found it to work very effectively in reducing fluid accumulation. On the strength of his argument, digitalis was introduced into formal pharmacopeia. It took another 14 years for John Ferriar, a physician practicing in Manchester, to sort out the ability of digitalis to increase the contraction of heart muscles and to understand that its diuretic effect on the kidney was secondary to this inotropic action. However, as standardizing dosages of digitalis remained difficult, the medication was rarely used until modern times.

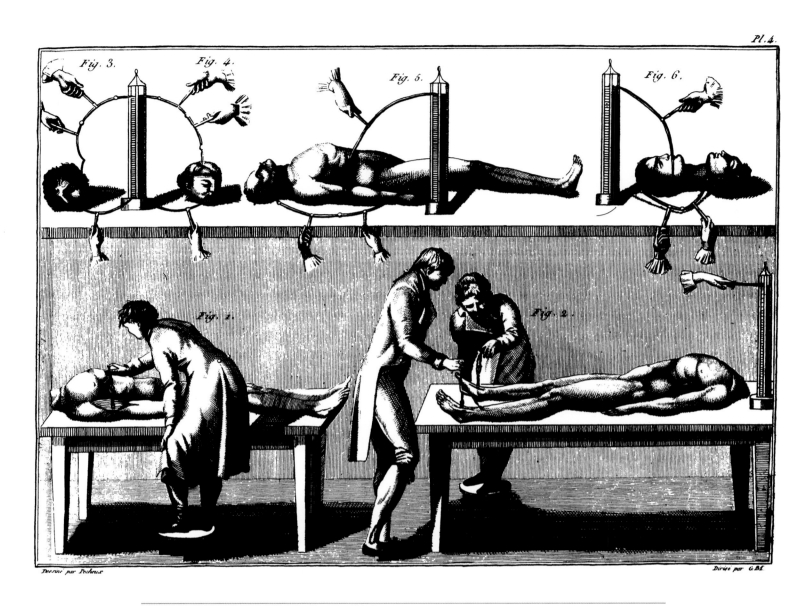

Though investigations into the nature and uses of electricity began earlier, it was in the late 18th and 19th centuries that medical applications were first tried. Some theoretically minded individuals wondered if the tingling, numbing, and occasional violent contractions produced by contact with electricity might have something to do with "the spark of life" and whether it might even be possible to bring about resuscitation through some use of electricity. But it was Luigi Galvani, a professor of obstetrics and anatomy at Bologna, who first demonstrated scientifically what he called "an indwelling of electricity" in animals through a series of experiments on frogs. Galvani published his finding in De Viribus Electritatis in Motu Musculari, that appeared in 1791. A decade later, his nephew, Jean Aldini, carried the idea further through experiments on executed criminals and found that the cadavers retained muscle irritability for two hours after death. Shown here is an illustration from Aldini's Essai Théoretic et Experimental Sur le Galvanism, published in 1804.

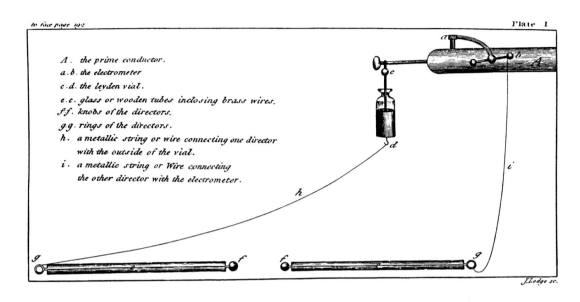

Plate I

A. *the prime conductor.*
a.b. *the electrometer*
c.d. *the leyden vial.*
e.e. *glass or wooden tubes inclosing brass wires.*
f.f. *knobs of the directors.*
g.g. *rings of the directors.*
h. *a metallic string or wire connecting one director*
with the outside of the vial.
i. *a metallic string or Wire connecting*
the other director with the electrometer.

J.Lodge sc.

Also dabbling in cardiac resuscitation were several Englishmen, including James Curry, M.D., and Charles Kite. Curry recommended using electrical shock only as a last resort, after all other methods were exhausted; and his writings reveal that when he did apply electricity to the dead, he had a remarkably good understanding of how the physician should rhythmically alternate shocks with pauses to allow inflation of the lungs. Kite's interest in resuscitation stemmed from his membership in the benevolent Royal Humane Society of London, which was devoted to the work of salvaging human life, including that of persons suddenly dead of drowning or asphyxiation. Citing personal knowledge of a youngster who had died after a fall and been resuscitated nearly a half hour later through electrical shocks to the thorax, Kite concluded that electricity might be capable of reproducing the motion of the heart and restarting circulation. Kite went on to devise a primitive "ventricular defibrillator" applied to the chest and powered by an electrostatic generator, which he described in his Essay Upon the Recovery of the Apparently Dead, 1788. As his illustration shows, the instrument consisted of "two pieces of brass wire, each two feet long, enclosed in glass tubes or wooden cases well varnished with knobs at one end, and rings at the other: the knobs are to be applied like common directors, to those parts between which we intend the [electric] fluid to pass; and one ring connected with a chain or metallic string, coming from the electrometer, and the other with a chain joined to the outside of the vial, which will be more convenient if suspended on the prime conductor." In this way, Kite said, shocks could be sent through any part of the body, their direction constantly changing, without putting the defibrillator's operator at risk. Another mode of resuscitation was suggested by an anonymous experimenter calling himself Dr. Sanctis. His so-called "Re-animation Chair" was supposed to generate electrical shocks by means of a voltaic pile to parts of the body, including the heart and diaphragm; the chair was also equipped with a bellows and laryngeal tube to inflate the lungs. Whether it was, in fact, ever tried successfully is not recorded.

John Wesley, the celebrated founder of Methodism, is seldom cited for his interest
in the medical uses of electricity, but he did in fact write the first book in English
on the subject. In Desideratum or Electricity Made Plain and Simple, published
in 1759, Reverend Wesley declared that electricity was nothing less than the "soul
of the Universe." Just as "the great machine of the World" derives its energy from
the Sun, its heart, so he reasoned that electricity played a part in maintaining
the body and human heart. "Electricity gives and preserves a proper Tone to the
Vessels. It promotes all Secretions, keeping every Part in Motion: It pervades the
whole Animal System, producing great variety of Effects…"

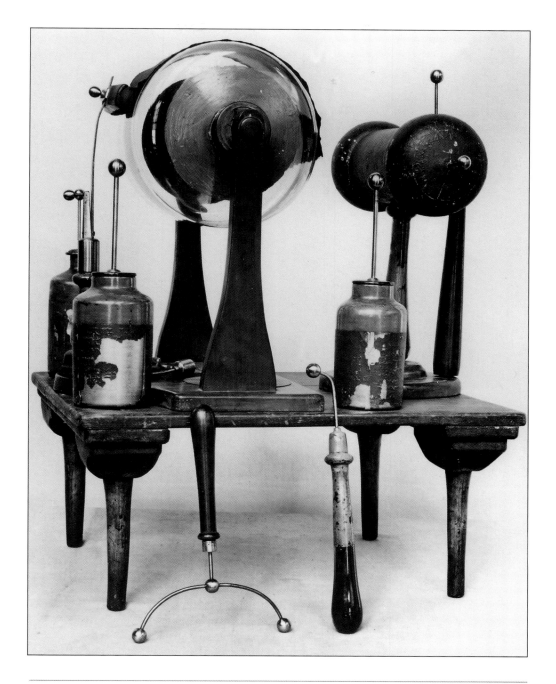

Regarding electricity's effect on circulation, the Reverend noted that the application of an electrical impulse to the body can quicken the pulse. This led him to believe that electrotherapy might be used to treat gout, kidney stones, headache, sciatica, rheumatism, angina pectoris, and heart palpitations. Wesley, who occasionally treated members of his congregation in this manner, used an electrostatic generator and a Leyden jar to produce the electric charge by which his "cures" were effected. While Wesley never achieved a scientific understanding of the therapies proposed, electrotherapy continues to be among the treatments recommended for several of these conditions at the end of the 20th century. A more persuasive case for medical electricity was made by British chemist Joseph Priestly, whose History and Present State of Electricity appeared in 1767. One of the experimental devices by which Priestly generated his electricity is the portable machine shown here. It consists of a rotating glass plate that produces an electrical charge, a set of Leyden jars that store the charge, and various connector-conductors, all assembled on an insulating stool.

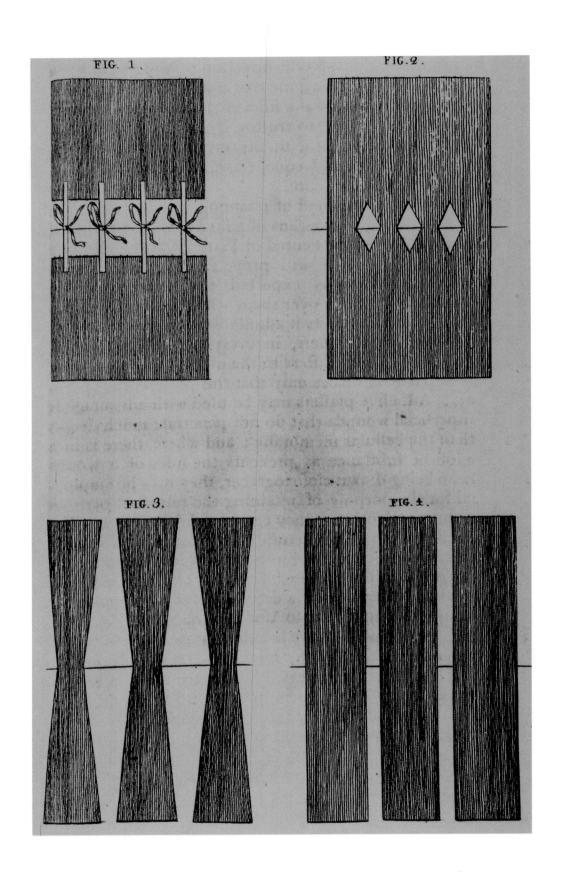

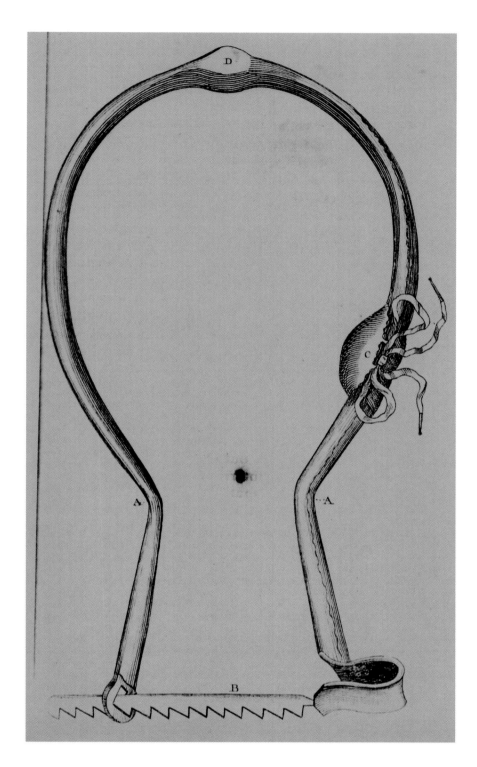

18th century surgeons had neither anesthesia nor aseptic methods by which to make the patient's role more comfortable and less hazardous. Their success rate depended to a significant degree on how quickly they could invade the conscious body and get out. Great store was consequently put on improved surgical tools and their proper use. One Scottish physician who devoted considerable attention to the matter was Benjamin Bell, whose six-volume System of Surgery found a particularly eager audience when the first American edition was published in Worcester, Massachusetts, in 1791. Shown here are two of the many tools Bell recommended. They are: several bandages and suture techniques (far left), and a hinged, ratcheting clamp for applying pressure to reduce hemorrhaging.

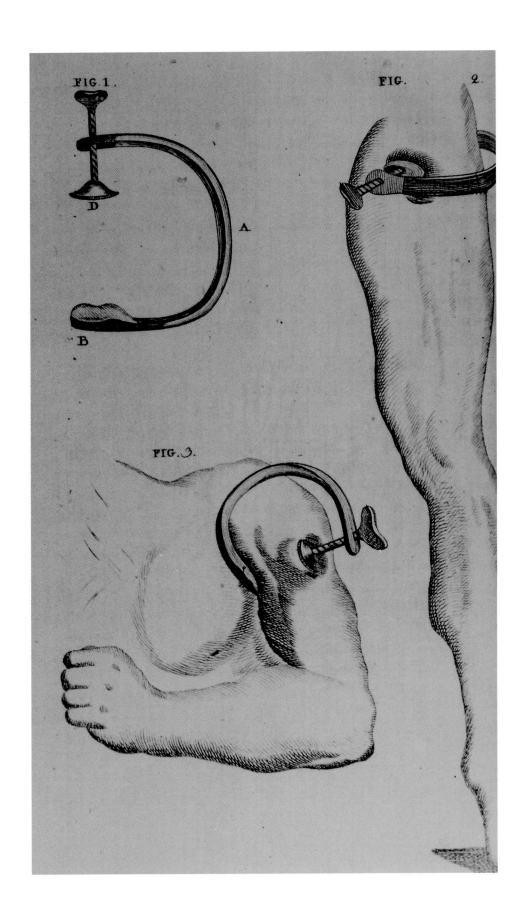

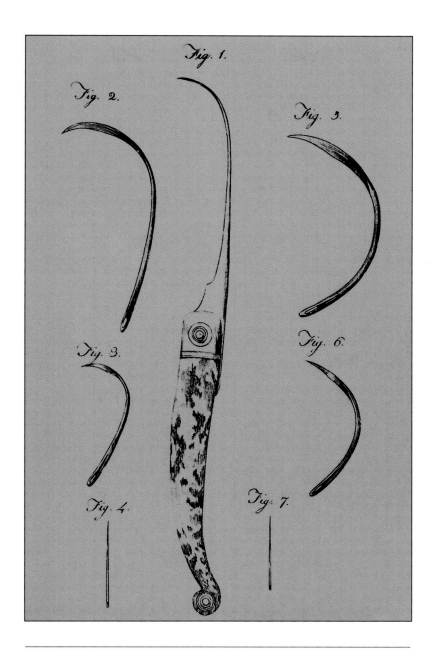

Demonstrated here are more of the tools recommended by Bell: the compression clamp (left); and several suturing needles together with a folding tortoise-handled probe for suturing (above). Not shown is suturing thread, which in these years was variously linen, fine silk thread, or cat gut.

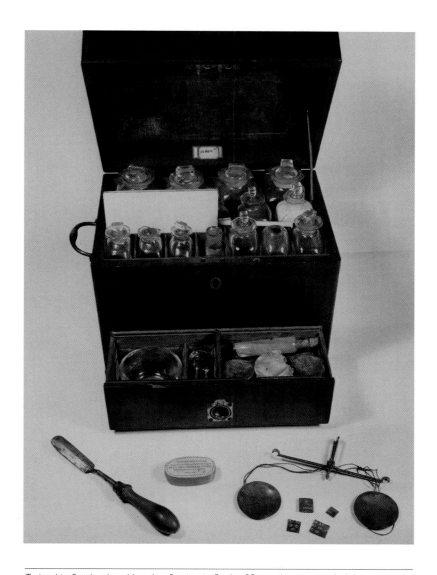

Trained in Scotland and London, Benjamin Rush of Pennsylvania provided the principal conduit for mid-18th century European medicine into America. He became the most influential physician on this side of the Atlantic, with his teachings extending well beyond his own life span. A signer of the Declaration of Independence, Rush taught chemistry and medicine at the University of Pennsylvania. In 1786 he founded the Philadelphia Dispensary, the first outpatient clinic for the poor in the nation. As befitted his time, Rush was an enthusiastic practitioner of "heroic medicine." His specific approach was based largely upon the tenets of the contemporary English theorist John Brown, who classified all diseases as either "sthenic" (caused by an excess of stimulation) or "asthenic" (an insufficiency of stimulation). Like most of his professional contemporaries, Rush believed in massive bloodletting—up to six to eight pints of blood might be drained over two days—as the best medicine for many complaints, heart trouble included. For those victims suffering from hypertension, a condition not yet recognized as pathological, such treatments could in fact bring some temporary relief. Some of the instruments Rush might use to perform a phlebotomy, or vein opening, to bleed his patients were similar to the lancets, scarifiers, and cups shown in his medical chest, above.

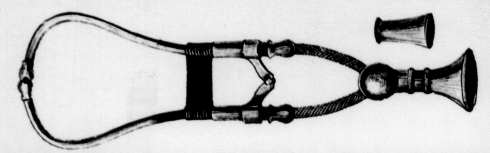

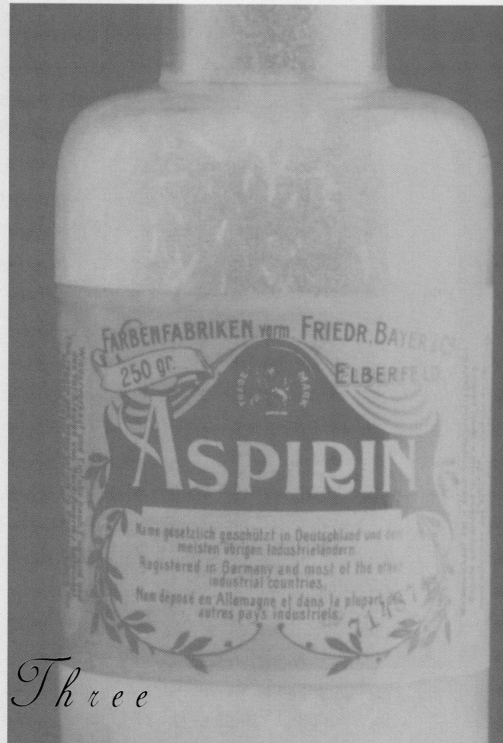

Chapter Three

GETTING DOWN TO BASICS

With the arrival of the 19th century many basic questions regarding the heart and the circulatory system began to be explored on their own terms. Underlying these developments were the emergence of pathology, experimental physiology, and surgery as separate specialties within the larger field of medical science. At the same time, a host of practical, inexpensive, and reliable new diagnostic tools and techniques became available—among them the stethoscope, the blood pressure monitor, and the oral thermometer providing the practicing physician with some objective measures of just how sick the patient was.

In pathology, investigations moved beyond Morgagni's essential descriptions of disease states to examine their underlying causes. This work received an enormous boost in 1839 when two Germans, botanist Matthias Schleiden and zoologist Theodor Schwann, established the cellular basis of all living organisms. Their revelations set the stage for Karl von Rokitansky of Vienna and the younger Rudolf Virchow of Berlin to step forward. von Rokitansky, a nonpracticing physician who devoted his career to morbid anatomy and pathology, systematically classified the changes in the heart and other organs, providing students with an unprecedented view of the progressive effects of disease processes. Virchow, also a pathologist by calling but a scientist of larger compass than von Rokitansky, used his skills as a microscopist to link pathological processes to fundamental changes in individual cells. So exhaustive were Virchow's arguments, so detailed the proofs, that his pronouncements were widely regarded as beyond dispute.

One of Virchow's colleagues went so far as to dub him the "Pope" of European medicine in recognition of the respect he was accorded within the profession.

Physiology also came of age in the 19th century, as Haller's 18th century mechanistic theories gave way to more detailed studies of particular organs and organ systems. Charting this new course in France was François Magendie, the self-described "rag picker in science." Magendie never held an academic position, but his tireless investigations led him to prove, among other important discoveries, that in the spinal cord the dorsal spinal root carries sensory impulses, and the anterior root carries motor messages. Magendie was followed, in turn, by his countryman Claude Bernard, a one-time playwright who returned to school to study medicine. Bernard's discoveries soon took him well beyond explanations of individual body systems to proposing a general theory of how the body works. Bernard argued that all of life's processes take place in an internal milieu and that it is a function of all biological systems to seek constant conditions within that environment. Bernard argued further that each system acts autonomously to maintain this equilibrium by means of self-adjusting mechanisms, the blood vessels expanding or constricting to maintain a constant body temperature and so on.

Meanwhile in Germany, physiology was dominated by Ernst Weber and Karl Ludwig. Ludwig's contributions to physiology are especially celebrated, first, because of his own brilliance in the field and, second, because of his generosity in promoting the groundbreaking work of the many fine pupils who came out of his Physiological Institute in Leipzig. Ludwig showed a particular originality in devising means to study the heart and circulation. His kymograph, a sensitive device capable of inscribing on paper a record of variations in blood pressure, was followed by the stromuhr, a tool for measuring blood flow. Ludwig also contributed monographs on the theoretical possibilities of keeping an organism alive through artificial perfusion, on the effect of temperature on heartbeat, on the depressor nerve of the heart, on auscultation of the heart, and on the location of the vasomotor control center in the medulla.

In surgery, which was still largely limited to sewing up open wounds and amputating severely damaged extremities, two major events occurred during these years to expand the surgeon's possibilities: the development of anesthesia and the introduction of asepsis and antisepsis. Of the two, anesthesia, which was dramatically introduced by William Morton in Boston in 1846, had the more immediate effect. Soon, surgeons everywhere felt free to undertake more ambitious and time-consuming surgical procedures, because they no longer had to cope with the screams of patients suffering intolerable pain. While surgeons were still reluctant to operate on the heart, circumstances such as battlefield injuries brought the more daring among them very close indeed. The second breakthrough, which began as passive antisepsis and gradually expanded to the more rigorous asepsis, had more far-reaching implications: It greatly reduced the mortality rates traceable to hospital infections. Antisepsis came into fashion as the result of Scotsman Joseph Lister's decision in 1865 to use a misting of weak carbolic acid to create an "antiseptic curtain" around surgical patients. As Lister wrote shortly after, mortality rates in his hospital's surgical wards fell promptly from 45 to 15 percent. By the last quarter of the century, every reputable hospital was making an effort to follow his example.

Electricity, which had made its first serious appearance as an adjunct of medicine in the previous century, continued to attract experimenters. A few physicians pursued its use as a therapeutic tool for heart disorders, particularly as an alternative to ligation and compression in treating traumatic aneurysms. Known as "galvano-puncture," this procedure involved plunging a pair of fine gold or platinum needles into the hemorrhaging bulge at right angles. Several minutes of electrical current were then applied via the crossed needles in the hope that the resulting heat would cause a clot to form and seal the leak. Mild full-body electricity was also tried as one more method of stimulating persons suffering from general debility, including "tired heart."

Lastly, the science of pharmacology was born as pharmacists began to correlate findings in the chemistry laboratory with known pathologies and the alterations they caused in normal function. Now it was possible to prescribe medications on a rational basis rather than by guess or instinct and to isolate active ingredients, either from the plant tissues in which they were hidden or to devise synthetic compounds similar to natural chemicals but superior to them in action. Patients continued to be besieged by the extravagant promises of some patent medicine manufacturers, but gradually a measure of order and ethical standards were brought to the industry, first on the Continent and in England and considerably later in the United States. The American Pharmacy Association, an organization which would become the institutional core of pharmacy's modern development in the United States, was founded in 1852. By the last quarter of the 19th century, most of today's major pharmaceutical houses were established and prospering. While few drugs of genuine use to heart patients had yet been singled out, digitalis was a notable exception; after having been largely overlooked since Withering's endorsement, it gained a second life at mid century in England and made its first appearance as a recommended therapeutic in the official *U.S. Pharmacopeia* of 1870.

STETHOSCOPES, CHEST, TONSIL, THROAT, MOUTH, NOSE AND EAR INSTRUMENTS.

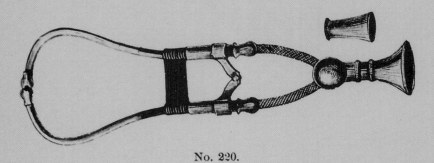

No. 220.

Camman's Double Stethoscope..$3 00

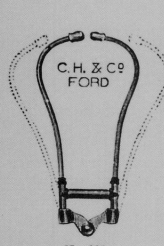 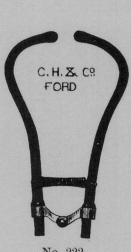 

No. 221.   No. 222.   No. 227.

Camman's Double Stethoscope, Camman's Double Stethoscope, Flint's
 with covered spring, $5 00.   hard rubber, $3 00.   Hammer,
Ditto, with open spiral spring,   75c.
   $4 00.

No.
223. Stethoscopes, cedar, plain...$ 50
224. "   ebony.. 75
225. "   " sectional... 1 50
226. "   hard rubber and elastic tube. 1 50
227. Percussion Hammer and Plessimeter Flints........................... 1 00
   Soft Rubber Ends for Camman's Stethoscopes........................ 25
228. Dr. Toboldt's large nickel-plated Laryngoscope, $25 00; and large-
    size Student's Lamp included, $32 50; or with Stand for Gas all
    complete, Tubing, Goose Neck, etc................................. 40 00
   Toboldt's small, not plated, $16 00; with Student's Lamp.............. 22 50
   Lamps, separate, plated... 7 50

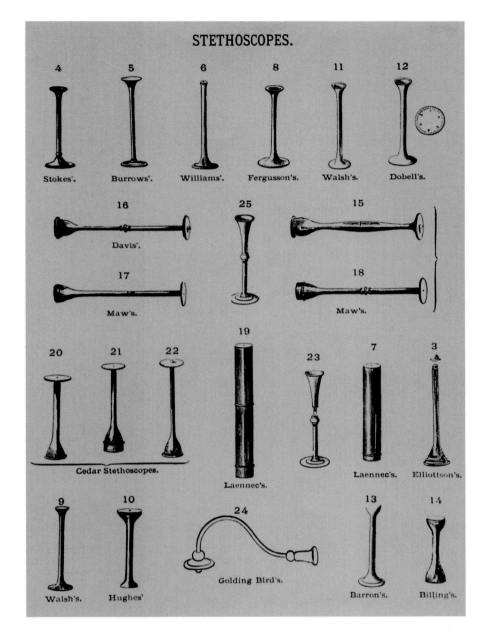

STETHOSCOPES.

4 — Stokes'.
5 — Burrows'.
6 — Williams'.
8 — Fergusson's.
11 — Walsh's.
12 — Dobell's.

16 — Davis'.
25
15

17 — Maw's.
18 — Maw's.

20
21
22
Cedar Stethoscopes.

19 — Laennec's.

23

7 — Laennec's.
3 — Elliottson's.

9 — Walsh's.
10 — Hughes'

24 — Golding Bird's.

13 — Barron's.
14 — Billing's.

Critical to the more effective treatment of heart disease was the development of better diagnostic tools. First came a technique called percussion, which was devised by Austrian physician Leopold Auenbrugger and made popular by Nicolas Corvisart, Napoleon Bonaparte's personal physician. Percussion was a technique by which a doctor might tap the chest with his finger and, with his ear against the thoracic cavity, listen for the sounds emanating. Frenchman René Laënnec was accustomed to using this technique, but he found it limited, especially when diagnosing corpulent patients. As he described it, "In 1816 I was consulted by a young woman laboring under general symptoms of a diseased heart and in whose case percussion and the application of the hand were of little avail on account of the great degree of fatness. I happened to recollect a simple and well-known fact in acoustics and fancied at the same time that it might be turned to some use on the present occasion… Immediately, on this suggestion, I rolled a quire of paper into a (tight) sort of cylinder and applied one end of it to the region of the heart and the other to my ear and was not a little surprised and pleased to find that I could thereby perceive the action of the heart in a manner much more clear and distinct than I had ever been able to do by the immediate application of the ear." Laënnec had devised "mediate auscultation." He went on to design a rigid wooden stethoscope similar to those shown in this physician's catalog. Laënnec also provided a new terminology related to the internal "lub-dubs" of the heart and their use in the differential diagnosis of various heart and lung diseases. Laënnec's stethoscope was superseded by a flexible-tube stethoscope, invented by C.W. Pennock of Philadelphia in 1839, and the more sound-sensitive binaural stethoscope with flexible tubes (shown on the opposite page) which appeared in 1855. The latter is attributed to George Cammann, M.D., of New York.

For many centuries, all cases of dropsy, or edema, were treated as a single condition with bleeding being the principal therapeutic response. Here, in a satirical print by James Gillray titled "Breathing a Vein" published in 1804, doubts as to the usefulness of this solution are evident on the faces of both patient and doctor. Two decades later, in 1827, the confusion was rectified when British physician Richard Bright elucidated the distinction between cardiac dropsy and renal dropsy, making different treatments of the conditions possible.

Englishman James Hope, chief of internal medicine at St. George's Hospital, London, made great advances in the diagnosis of acquired heart defects during the first half of the 19th century. His book, Diseases of the Heart and Great Vessels *(1831)*, became a standard in the treatment of heart and circulatory conditions for many years. Hope was the first medical authority to write specifically on the subject of the heart murmur, a diagnosis more easily made in living patients through physicians' growing skills with the stethoscope.

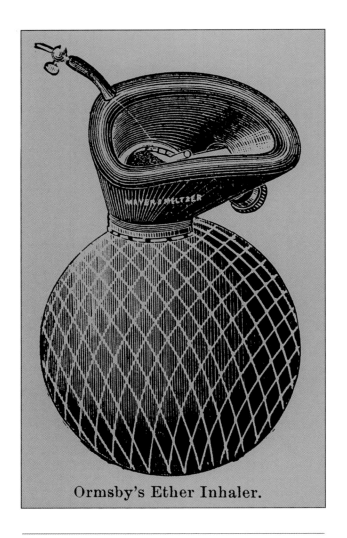

Ormsby's Ether Inhaler.

Until surgeons were equipped with anesthesia, most forms of surgery were extremely difficult for everyone involved. This began to change with the introduction of several soporifics in the 1840s. Ether was first discovered by Samuel Guthrie, a Massachusetts physician, in 1831, but for years it was regarded as a chemical curiosity of no practical use. It was first applied in surgery by Georgia physician Crawford Long in 1842, but failure to publish his breakthrough technique allowed the credit to go to dentist William Morton. Morton demonstrated ether's use in 1846 before a group of amazed physicians at Massachusetts General Hospital in Boston. Nitrous oxide, or "laughing gas," was first tried in Massachusetts about this time, too. And Scottish physician James Simpson began using chloroform in 1847, though he was roundly condemned for doing the devil's work. By 1858, when the engraving of a chloroform inhaler shown at right was published in Britain, the idea of using gaseous substances to make patients insensitive to pain was firmly established on both sides of the Atlantic. The process was named "anesthesia," a term coined by America's own Oliver Wendell Holmes. The bulbous device, above, was a somewhat simpler, hand-held ether inhaler from the same era.

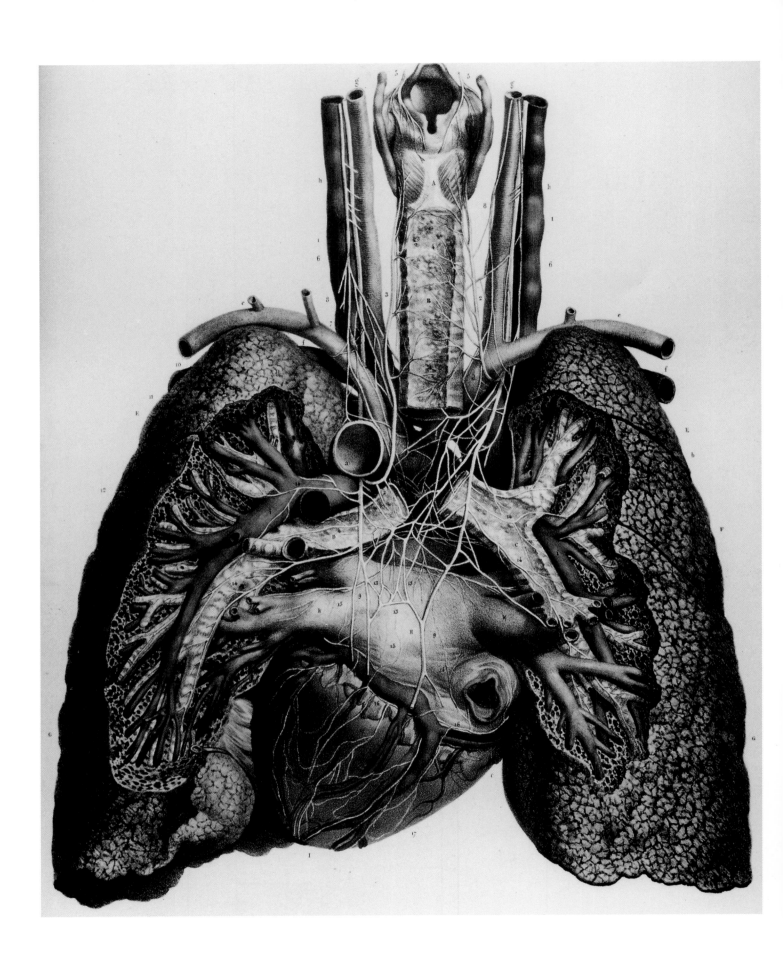

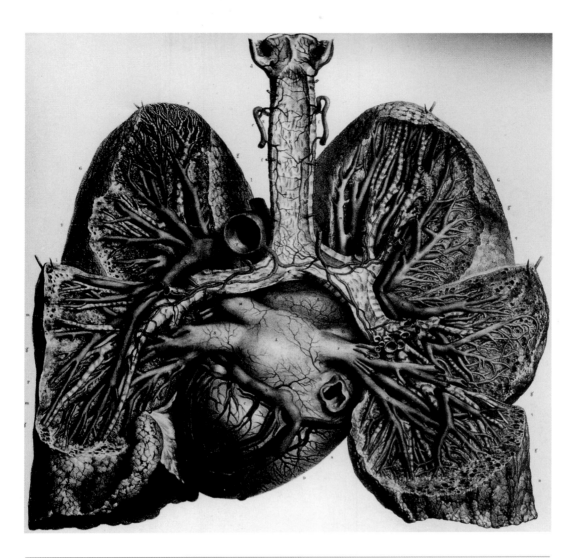

It took two decades for French surgeon Marc Jean Bourgery and his artist-collaborator Nicolas Henri Jacob to complete their massive Atlas of Anatomy and Surgery. The last of the 726 hand-colored, life-size lithographs was done shortly before 1854 when Volume Eight was published. The collaboration was exceptionally fruitful, as the two plates from Volume Four showing the heart, lungs, and major vessels demonstrate. They record an extraordinary mastery of detail with an artistic flair that had not been seen since Vesalius' work.

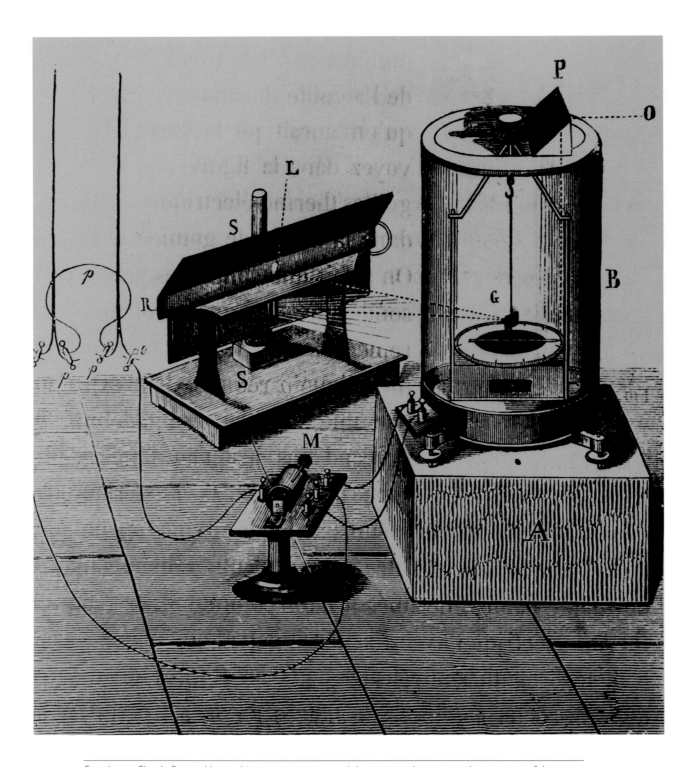

Frenchman Claude Bernard began his career as a poet and dramatist and went on to become one of the true giants of experimental pathology. Among his many major studies was his work on the role of sympathetic nerves in regulating metabolism and body temperature. Through his findings he identified the regulatory function of vasoconstrictor and vasodilator nerves in 1858. While this information had a bearing on the mechanism of all involuntary muscles in the body, it had particularly critical significance in the understanding of the action of the heart. Shown here is one of the devices Bernard used to measure temperature changes occurring in an organism as the result of applying electrodes to a sympathetic nerve. When he found that the temperature dropped, he was able to deduce that the sympathetic nerve caused dilation.

Ernst Weber, shown here in an 1845 daguerreotype, was one of three Weber brothers to distinguish themselves in physiology. Ernst was professor of anatomy and physiology at Leipzig when he made medical history in 1845 by isolating the specific cranial nerves responsible for controlling heart action. Assisted by his younger brother Edouard, he brought the heart of a frog to a standstill by placing one pole of an electromagnetic apparatus in the frog's nostril and the other on a cross-section of the frog's spinal cord at the level of the fourth vertebra. The Webers subsequently localized the site of activity to the vagus nerve, and later found a similar effect among warm-blooded animals, including humans. The Weber brothers also collaborated on Hydrodynamics of Wave-Motion, *in which they measured the velocity of pulse waves and showed that the pulse is not synchronous in all arteries but varies according to the circumference of the vessel and its distance from the heart.*

The first academic chair of the new science of pathology in France was occupied by Jean Cruveilhier. The Paris professor is remembered as the first medical scientist to describe disseminated sclerosis, the condition known today as atherosclerosis. Cruveilhier fell short of interpreting its causes believing it to be simply a manifestation of phlebitis or inflammation. He was correct, however, in reversing a long-held theory that "senile" gangrene was the arteries' means of self-protection against hemorrhage prior to the "spontaneous" dropping away of a limb. He showed that gangrene occurred as the result of arterial occlusion and, more particularly, of dense blood clots.

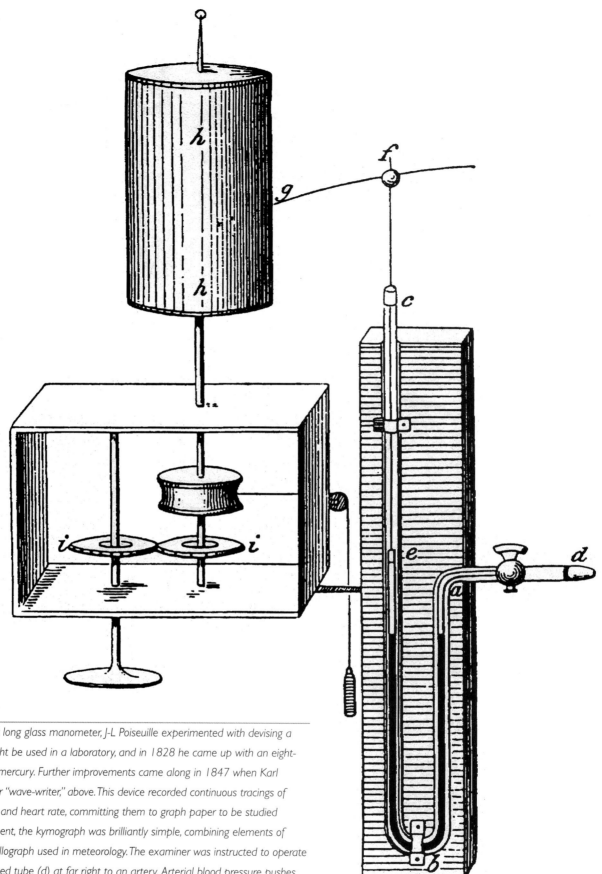

Inspired by Stephen Hales' nine-foot long glass manometer, J-L Poiseuille experimented with devising a more practical manometer that might be used in a laboratory, and in 1828 he came up with an eight-inch long U-shaped tube filled with mercury. Further improvements came along in 1847 when Karl Ludwig developed the kymograph, or "wave-writer," above. This device recorded continuous tracings of systolic and diastolic blood pressure and heart rate, committing them to graph paper to be studied and analyzed. As a piece of equipment, the kymograph was brilliantly simple, combining elements of Poiseuille's manometer with the oscillograph used in meteorology. The examiner was instructed to operate it as follows: First, attach the U-shaped tube (d) at far right to an artery. Arterial blood pressure pushes the mercury to rise in the glass column (e) causing a light float atop the column (f) to move up and down, moving the fine wire scribe attached at the same time. The tip of the scribe (g) rests lightly on a rotating drum (h) covered with paper blackened with soot. A simple system of clock gears below, driven by the gravitational pull of a weight and controlled by the escapement, causes the drum to rotate at a constant speed. The record, inscribed as a white scratch on the blackened paper, is then removed from the drum, the paper varnished to keep it from smudging, and examined in detail. Ludwig once referred to these early tracings as "the first stammerings of the heart."

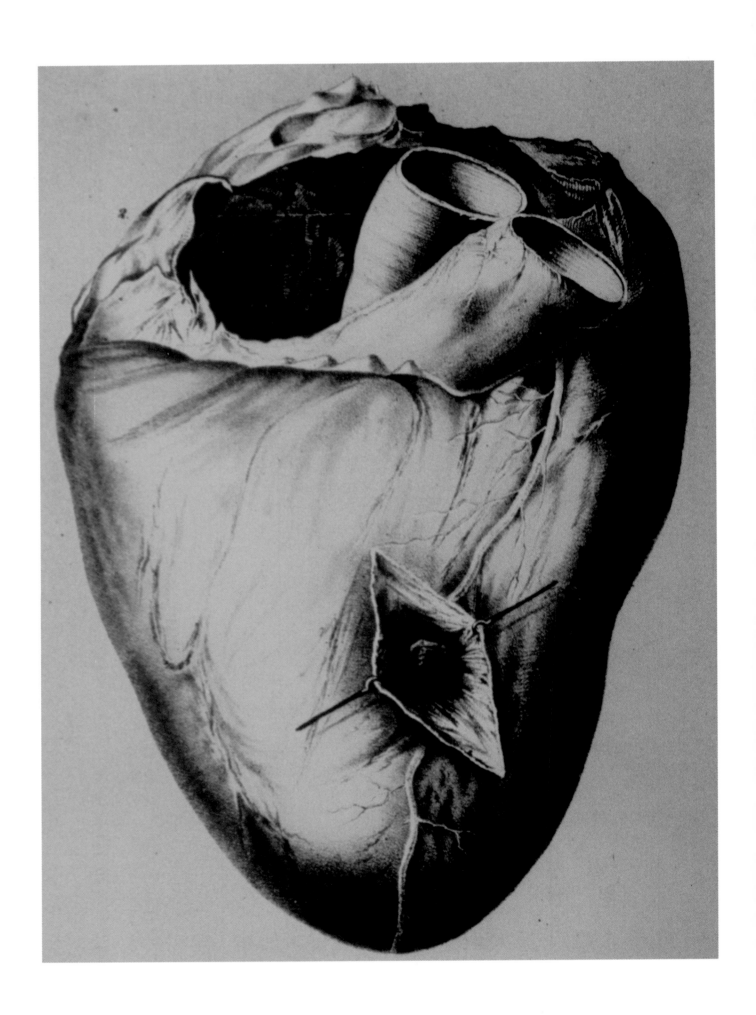

Rudolf Virchow was appointed professor of pathology at the University of Berlin in 1856 and concurrently director of the city's Pathological Institute. He quickly rose to become a dominant figure in contemporary medicine, teaching generations of pathologists from all over Europe. Virchow's greatest and most lasting contribution, however, was the pioneering work set forth in his landmark text on cellular pathology, Die Cellularpathologie, 1858. In it Virchow stressed the concept that all living cells arise only from preexisting cells and that disease causes profound but identifiable changes in the structure and appearance of those cells. He made many important contributions to cardiology, including observations regarding thrombosis, embolism, and phlebitis. He also detected the link between cholesterol and arteriosclerosis through examinations of clogged arteries and the fatty deposits, or plaque, found there. Virchow was prescient enough to propose that injury to the inner wall of a blood vessel, possibly caused by fat, might lead to inflammation and secondary plaque formation, a notion very close to present theory.

John Murray Carnochan was a professor of surgery at New York Medical College as well a surgeon-in-chief at the State Emigrant Hospital on Ward's Island, New York. Noted for his daring, Carnochan is reported to have performed the first excision of the superior maxillary nerve for the treatment of facial neuralgia in 1858 and to have ligated the carotid arteries on both sides as a means of treating elephantiasis in 1867. Perhaps his most ambitious effort, however, was his attempt to treat a gunshot wound to the heart. He undertook this risky and ultimately unsuccessful procedure c. 1857. He subsequently published its details in the American Medical Monthly, from which the illustration at the left was taken. Though direct surgical attempts upon the heart never succeeded in those years, physicians continued to hope that they would eventually find a way. Certainly, the experience of opening the wounded chest and reporting on the nature of the damage suffered by the heart muscle, added to the growing literature of knowledge about the heart.

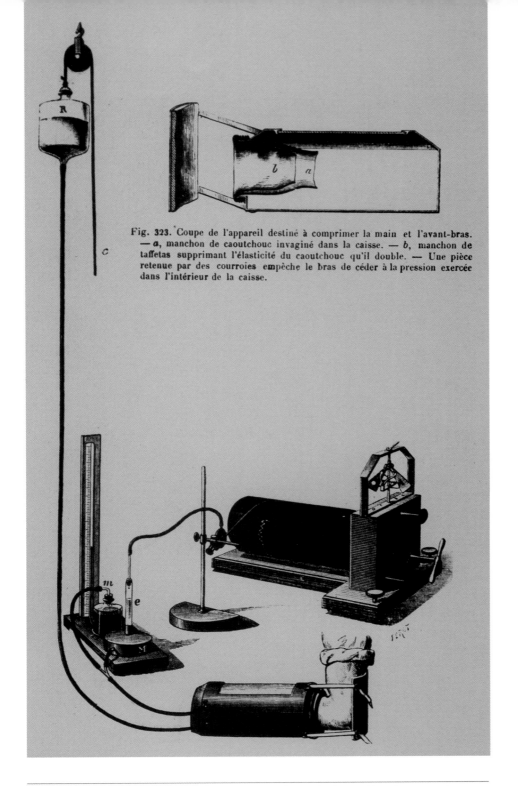

Fig. 323. Coupe de l'appareil destiné à comprimer la main et l'avant-bras. — *a*, manchon de caoutchouc invaginé dans la caisse. — *b*, manchon de taffetas supprimant l'élasticité du caoutchouc qu'il double. — Une pièce retenue par des courroies empêche le bras de céder à la pression exercée dans l'intérieur de la caisse.

"Marey's tambour," as the sphygmograph was sometimes known, had several ingenious parts. A pneumatic sleeve, not unlike the modern pressure cuff, consisting of layers of rubber and taffeta, enclosed the hand and forearm snugly. Hollow tubes ran from the cuff to transmit pressure changes indirectly to the stylus. Improvements in Marey's design followed soon, with Scipione Riva-Rocci's prototype of the modern instrument appearing in 1896. Later, Nikolai Korotkoff developed the auscultory method of pulse-taking: instead of feeling for the pulse to determine systolic-pressure endpoints, Korotkoff proposed using the stethoscope at the pit of the elbow for more accurate readings. In the process, Korotkoff also found he could detect diastolic pressure as well.

French pathologist Étienne-Jules Marey devised the first practical instrument for measuring arterial pressure, amplitude, duration, and compressibility when he produced the sphygmograph, the ancestor of the modern sphygmomanometer, in 1860. Marey, who was a talented tinkerer as well as a medical man, went on to develop a camera that took many pictures of the same scene in rapid sequence. This predecessor of the motion picture camera (which he invented for his own use several years ahead of Thomas Edison) was constructed as a means to learn about animal locomotion, another scientific interest.

Karl von Rokitansky, a Czech, rose to become head of the department of pathological anatomy at the Vienna Institute of Pathology and one of the best-known morbid anatomists of his day. He is said to have personally performed some 30,000 postmortems in his 50-year career, the results of which he published in various editions of his classic Handbook of Pathological Anatomy beginning in 1842. von Rokitansky is shown here in a photograph taken by Aaron Friedenwald, a Baltimore physician who trained with him in Vienna.

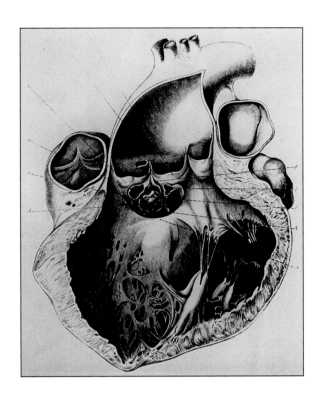

Among von Rokitansky's finest works in pathological anatomy were those devoted to the heart and circulatory system. The first of these was a monograph on diseases of the arteries, published in 1852 and illustrated with 23 folio plates. The second, issued in 1875, was the result of 14 years of study and was devoted to defects in the septum of the heart. These illustrations were taken from the latter publication.

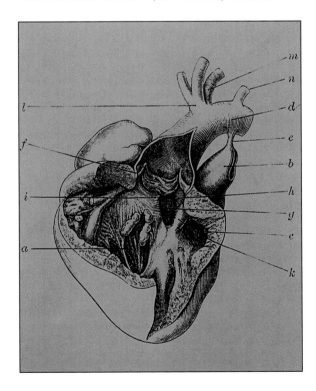

Above: Austin Flint, Sr. was sometimes called "the American Laënnec" by his contemporaries, for he was a great popularizer of auscultation and other techniques of physical diagnosis applied to the heart. Dr. Flint, a voice of moderation in all things medical, noted that performing the necessary steps of a physical examination was becoming increasingly more difficult, as Victorian-era patients, women especially, were reluctant to bare their skin to the probing and percussion of the physician.

Left: Englishman Thomas Lauder Brunton early demonstrated an interest in the action of drugs on the heart, writing his dissertation on digitalis prior to graduating from the medical school in Edinburgh in 1868. Brunton went on to study pathology with Karl Ludwig in Leipzig. He returned to become a physician at St. Bartholomew's, London, where he published a series of notable papers on the relationships between chemical structures and physiological actions. In 1867 Brunton introduced the novel recommendation that amyl nitrite (nitroglycerin), a vasodilator as well as a component of explosives, was effective in treating angina pectoris. He rightly based his prescription on the argument that angina resulted from the heart's starvation for blood caused by a narrowing of the vessels.

In an illustration from Harper's Weekly, 1874, physicians and observers cluster at the bedside of a sick woman at the Hôpital de la Pitie, Paris, as blood is transfused directly from the spurting artery of a healthy man into a tube inserted into the patient's arm. As was typical of the era, the doctors are dressed in their street clothes, and no effort at antisepsis of any kind is visible. This kind of human-to-human transfusion was by no means the rule: the author of a contemporary medical review stated that among the 478 transfusions for which he was able to find documentation since the procedure's first use in 1667, sheep and other animals were used in one quarter of the procedures. The author also reported that clinical improvement was observed in roughly one-third of patients who received animal blood. He claimed that about one-half of those receiving human blood responded favorably. Considering that the existence of blood types as a complicating factor was not yet recognized, these figures are surprisingly favorable and probably inaccurate.

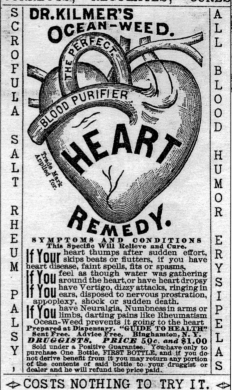

Though advances were being made in the scientific development of drugs to treat heart conditions, most patients in the 19th century continued to self-medicate from an ever-growing supply of nonprescription patent medicines. As governments and medical establishments were slow to exercise control over what manufacturers put into their medications or the extravagant promises made for them, concoctions ranged from benign and ineffective to potent and often dangerous. Shown here are advertising handouts for two of the many medications claiming to improve the workings of the heart. Dr. Kilmer's Ocean-Weed Heart Remedy was produced in Binghamton, NY. The manufacturer claimed it to be a specific for heart thumps, irregular beats, flutters, faint spells, fits and spasms, vertigo, edema, tinnitus, apoplexy, shock, numbness, darting pains, scrofula, and a variety of blood poisonings. Ocean-Weed was also said to "relieve and cure...sudden death," with a money-back guarantee. Burdock's Blood Bitters was less specific in its claims, though strengthening the blood was thought to be a good idea in general. Like many such restoratives, the active ingredients were likely to be a mix of herbs, alcohol, and very possibly a narcotic, either morphine or cocaine. Also shown here is aspirin, which was first synthesized by an Alsatian chemist in 1853 on the model of the natural painkiller salicylic acid found in willow bark. Aspirin was not produced commercially, however, until a German chemist employed by Friedrich Bayer & Co. developed it in tablet form in 1897, and the company went on to market aspirin as the analgesic shown here. Nearly a century later, aspirin's blood-thinning qualities were recognized as useful in the treatment of some forms of heart disease as well.

Burdock
Blood
Bitters

S. Weir Mitchell, M.D., trained under Claude Bernard in Paris and returned to Philadelphia to become the leading American neurologist of his time. Mitchell produced many astute papers on the physiology of the nervous system, but his lasting influence lay in his work in neurasthenia, or "nervous exhaustion," by which was understood conditions of depression and withdrawal. To treat such patients, who were principally female, Mitchell developed what he called the "rest cure," consisting of prolonged bedrest, gentle exercises, massage, electrical stimulation, a prescribed diet of mild foods, and removal from domestic and business cares. While Mitchell did not go so far as to recommend this therapeutic approach for the treatment of persons with heart disease, lack of better alternatives prompted some physicians to recommend the rest cure anyway on the premise that it could not hurt.

Weir Mitchell's rest cure had much in common with the hydrotherapeutic cures being offered in many mineral spas, especially in Europe. A preeminent center of curing was Bad Nauheim, northeast of Frankfurt, Germany. The resort was especially known for its carbonic acid and saline springs, believed to have a salutory effect on the heart and circulation. Physicians in America, who were unable to supply their patients with these waters, did the next best thing, which was to mix salts with hot water and offer so-called "Nauheim baths" in the office. This photo shows a treatment being given a heart patient in a New York doctor's office at the turn of the century.

Chapter Four

CROSSING THE GREAT DIVIDE

wo themes predominate in the history of heart medicine in the United States in the last quarter of the 19th century, the improvement of formal medical education and the emergence of the first imaging modality in Wilhelm K. Roentgen's x-ray machine.

U.S. medical training in the 1870s was widely regarded as unregulated and woefully substandard. Though efforts had been made in the previous century to follow the better examples available in Europe, the general American tendency toward decentralization and local rule had created a chaotic situation; men of every description—from the careful practitioner to the outright charlatan— were free to claim a medical degree and call themselves a doctor. State medical societies made periodic attempts to set up licensing standards, but they received little support from government institutions. A survey taken in one southern state in 1850 found that of 201 "doctors" interviewed, only 35 had graduated from a regular medical school and of the remainder, 97 had no formal training at all. They were, in other words, essentially self-taught, which meant that advances like antisepsis, clinical diagnostic techniques, and the responsible use of medications were likely to be lost on them. Daniel Drake, M.D., described the run-of-the-mill physician in his part of the Midwest as scarcely better prepared to heal patients than a scoundrel, "his medicines unlabeled, and thrown into a chaos, bundles untied and bottles left uncorked, or stopped with plugs of paper; dead flies in the ointment within his jars…his spatulas, foul and rusty; his surgical instruments oxidating and rusting away, like his mind…his floor spotted over with the blood of his surgical patients, and his own tobacco juice."

Even those men who made it through an organized medical school were likely to be poorly prepared. Training might last from a few weeks to a few months, following a curriculum that was typically out-of-date and incomplete. Any high-minded candidate who wanted training in the latest clinical practices or medical theories had no alternative but to go abroad—preferably to Paris, Berlin, Vienna, or Leipzig—for at least part, if not all, of his education. Between 1875 and 1914, an estimated 15,000 U.S. doctors-in-training did just that, exposing themselves in the process to the benefits of systematic clinical teaching as well as to the transforming influence that research was having on European teaching and medical practice.

But the problems inherent in the U.S. medical scene eventually provided its solution. These same European-trained physicians were becoming a dedicated and potent force for change. Beginning in the 1870s, they initiated a movement toward the radical restructuring of the American medical profession along European models and standards. The first real reform was made in 1871 by President Charles Eliot of Harvard, who lengthened the curriculum of Harvard Medical School to three years, introduced student grading, and provided better facilities for clinical and laboratory instruction. The medical departments of several other leading universities, including Pennsylvania, Syracuse, and Michigan, soon followed. And a new medical school and research center was created as an adjunct to Johns Hopkins Hospital in Baltimore when William Welch and others founded Johns Hopkins Medical School in 1893.

In designing its curriculum, Johns Hopkins' leaders raised the educational bar even higher: they required a college degree as a requisite for admission, offered a four-year graded curriculum, incorporated laboratory work into medical training, and integrated the college's facilities with those of the hospital to provide advanced students with ample on-site clinical training. Many of the most eminent medical men of the time were attracted to serve on Johns Hopkins' faculty, including Canada's celebrated Sir William Osler, who became the first physician-in-chief, neurologist Harvey Cushing, and surgeon William Halsted. Halsted, in instituting the resident system for training surgeons and teaching surgery over a 33-year career at the institution, became perhaps the most influential figure in surgery that America has ever produced.

As medical knowledge and the skills to implement it grew in complexity, many areas of medicine inevitably became compartmentalized. Increasingly, the more ambitious physicians were inclined to specialize, either in some aspect of clinical medicine—gynecology, ophthalmology, neurology, or endocrinology to name some of the fields that grew early on—or to choose some area of academic research and to remain within a university/hospital setting where the greatest opportunities for unusual cases lay. Academic physiologists, while they might pursue many interests, produced much of the most interesting discoveries in cardiovascular medicine in these years. As for anyone concentrating in the clinical treatment of patients with heart disease, the days of cardiac specialization still lay ahead.

One event that brought the time of specialization a little closer to realization was the discovery in 1895 of x-rays as a tool for observing the body's interior. Less than a year after Wilhelm K. Roentgen made his momentous announcement in Germany, Francis Williams of Boston read a paper before the Association of American Physicians on the use of radiography in diagnosing heart disease. He said he had examined a patient with an enlarged heart, managing to measure and thereby compare it with a normal heart, all without the patient having to remove two shirts and a waistcoat. Within the next three years, Williams grew in skill, using radiology to study and compile remarkably accurate descriptions of virtually all the recognized cardiac diseases, including intrathoracic aneurysm, cardiac hypertrophy, and pericardial effusion. He also compared percussion-determined and radiologically measured heart size with postmortem specimens in more than 500 cases and concluded that radiologic diagnosis was consistently more reliable and efficient than conventional methods. Lastly, Williams experimented with radiology's near relation, fluoroscopy, to make direct observations of the beating heart. Following Williams' example, many other physiologists and clinicians were inspired to investigate various methods of diagnostic imaging to see how it might improve their ability to treat heart disease.

As for surgical interventions in the heart itself, it seemed, for all the radical changes in other phases of heart treatment, that surgery was only marginally more advanced in the last quarter of the 19th century than it had been in the time of Galen. In 1895 a commentator on the medical scene wrote confidently that insofar as the heart was concerned, surgery had "probably reached the limits set by Nature: no new method and no new discovery can overcome the natural difficulties that attend a wound of the heart." Scarcely had he written these words than Ludwig Rehn, a professor of surgery in Frankfurt, Germany, performed the first successful suture of a torn heart. With this bold step, the era of cardiac surgery was born.

Beginning in the 1870s, medical schools began to teach the use of the stethoscope as a tool indispensable to the modern practitioner of medicine. Shown here is a classroom demonstration in the main amphitheater of the Chattanooga Medical College, Chattanooga, Tennessee, at the turn of the century. To judge from the visages of those in attendance, some of the listeners were physicians in mid-career, returning to learn the latest in techniques. Of the 50-odd students, only one was a woman, still a relative rarity in medical schools in the United States when this photograph was taken.

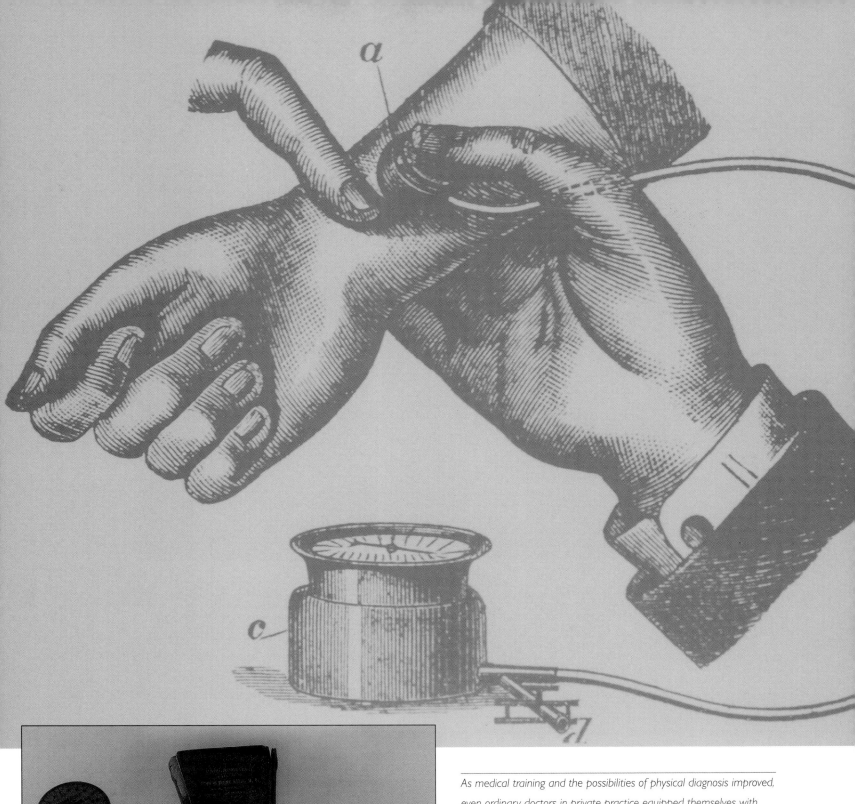

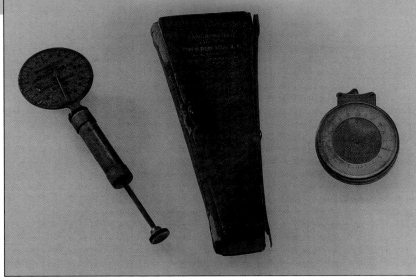

As medical training and the possibilities of physical diagnosis improved, even ordinary doctors in private practice equipped themselves with an assortment of basic tools. Shown here are two late 19th century sphygmomanometers with which to measure blood pressure. The small pocket version with case, variously referred to as a "pulse watch" or "tonometer," took crude readings of arterial pulse. A hair-trigger spring inside the device acted as a transducer, relaying the rise and fall of the broad-footed plunger over the throbbing artery. It was devised and patented by John Bethune Stein, M.D., of New York. The engraving above shows a somewhat more elaborate pneumatic device, also for taking wrist pulse. The device under the examiner's thumb rests on the radial artery; a tension screw (a) adjusts to pick up the beat, and the reading is sent via a pneumatic tube to the table-top device. It was offered in an 1883 medical catalog published in Vienna.

Before the last quarter of the 19th century, the supply of professional nurses to tend the acutely ill and those with chronic conditions such as heart disease was almost nonexistent, but then, virtually simultaneously, three preparatory schools were founded. The earliest was Bellevue Training School, which opened in New York City in May 1873, followed later that same year by Connecticut Training School in New Haven, Connecticut, and Massachusetts Training School in Boston. All three were modeled on the Florence Nightingale Plan in emphasizing science-based standards of sanitation, nutrition, and the sympathetic care of patients, but because it was first implemented at Bellevue, the curriculum came to be known in America as the "Bellevue System." Five young women enrolled the first year at the New York school with the understanding that they would train for 12 months and then serve a second 12 months before receiving their full credentials. Shown here are nursing students gathered in the parlor at Bellevue Hospital Nurses' Home in 1882 as they observe a lesson in bandaging techniques.

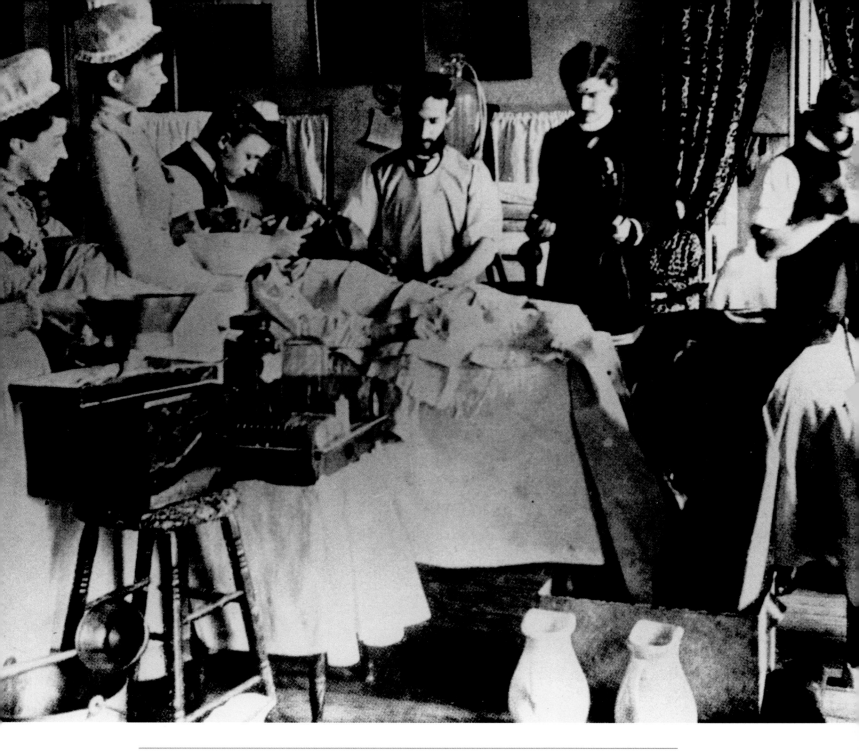

Bellevue nurses set the pattern for wearing sanitary uniforms rather than street clothes while on duty, a concept adopted only with reluctance. The trim uniforms consisted of a long blue seersucker dress with white apron, collar and cuffs, a white cap, and a pin identifying their school. So valuable did the services of the first trained nurses become that many hospitals founded their own programs. By the turn of the century, some 432 schools were in existence in the United States. Shown here are two newly minted Bellevue nurses assisting surgeons as they administer anesthesia c. 1880.

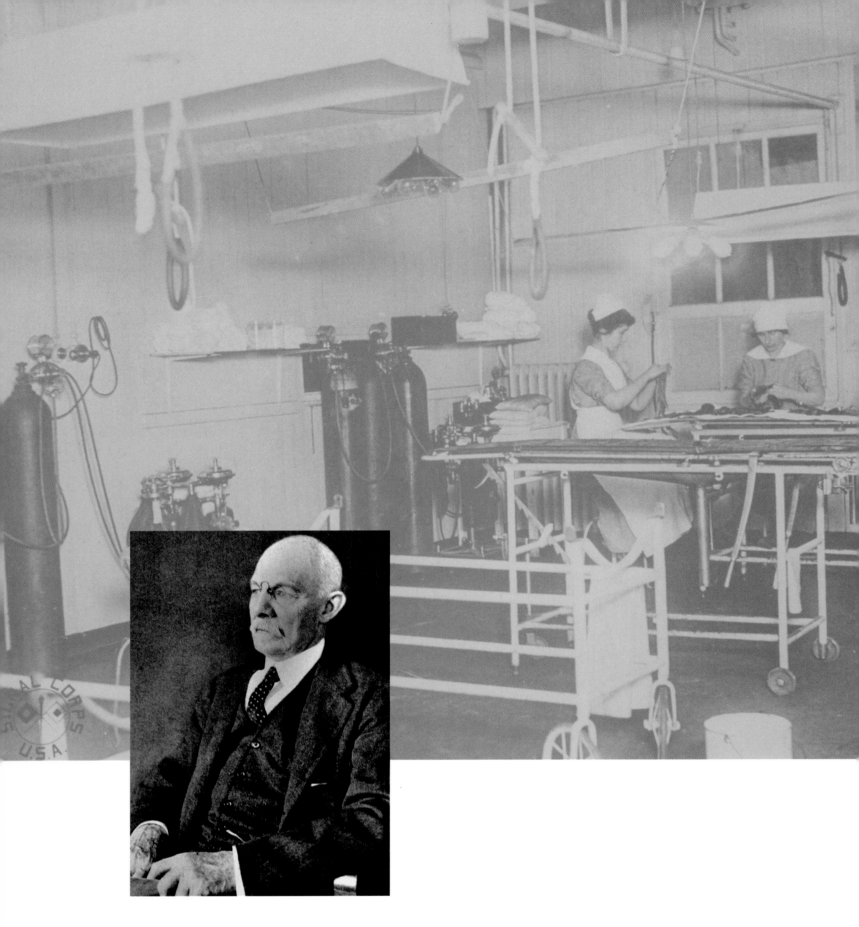

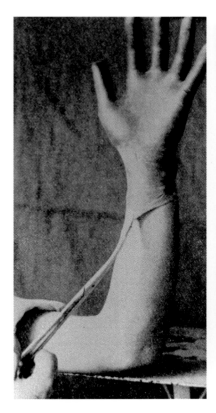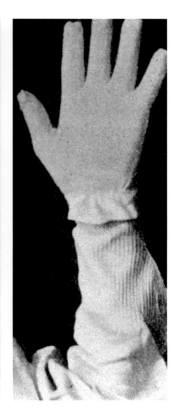

As a teacher, William Stewart Halsted brought a new level of technical ability to the practice of surgery in the United States. Over a long career spent chiefly at Johns Hopkins Medical School, he trained two generations of physicians in modern methods, and many of these same students went on to become prominent medical educators, carrying his methods and philosophy to other parts of the country. Halsted is particularly remembered for the emphasis he placed on precision dissections and suture techniques. That his methods were superior to others is demonstrated in a long list of "firsts" that are credited to his name. For example, in 1884 he performed the first refusion of a patient's own blood in a case of CO_2 poisoning; five years later he completed what was probably the first successful ligation of the left subclavian artery for a large aneurysm, a procedure that at least a dozen of his peers had failed at. As Halsted wrote on another occasion, the deft surgeon cannot help but find great drama in the moment of tying the ligature in such a situation: "The monstrous, booming tumor is stilled by a tiny thread, the tempest silenced by the magic wand." Halsted also did much to promote aseptic techniques, including the introduction of gutta-percha tissue in drainage and the use of rubber gloves as a sanitary measure in the operating room. Shown above are several models of the new-fangled gloves, as offered in a medical catalog some years later. In the left photo are two nurses mending well-used gloves.

The climate for experimentation and discovery in medicine only grew as time passed and the science of pathology developed. The command center of this activity in the United States was Johns Hopkins University Medical School, Baltimore, where this c. 1895 photograph of a graduate student at his bench microscope was taken. The first director of this laboratory was William Welch, who had received his training in Germany, where hospital-based pathology laboratories had been an established tradition for nearly half a century. Welch also made important studies of embolism and thrombosis.

Above: Posed in a doorway of Harvard Medical School are three éminences grises of American medicine at the turn of the century. They are, from left to right, John Collins Warren, Henry Pickering Bowditch, and an older Sir William Osler, who was there possibly as a guest lecturer. Warren taught pathology at Harvard Medical School for several decades and wrote two texts dealing with the heart and circulation. Bowditch is remembered as the first to describe two fundamental laws of cardiac physiology: the "treppe" or "staircase" phenomenon by which the cardiac muscle shows a successive increase in amplitude and the "all or none law" of cardiac contraction.

Right: Drs. Harvey Cushing, Howard Kelly, Sir William Osler, and William Sydney Thayer, seated forefront, were all members of Johns Hopkins Medical School's distinguished faculty when this classroom photo was taken in the 1890s. Thayer's contributions include observations on gonorrheal endocarditis and the first clinical notation of the third sound of the heart. Cushing is remembered as one of America's greatest neurological surgeons. Osler, who was a Canadian by birth, was the author of Principles and Practice of Medicine, which from its first edition in 1892 remained the most influential guide to modern medical treatment for several decades. Not shown, but another notable at Johns Hopkins in these years, was the Irish academic surgeon Henry Newell Martin. Martin made important strides toward the ultimate development of a heart-lung machine: in 1881 he isolated a mammalian heart, devised the means to perfuse fluids backward through its aorta toward the left ventricle and coronary arteries, and found that he could sustain the heart's viability for a time. Instructors at Johns Hopkins were understandably excited about the educational climate they found here. One spoke of "splendid times...no shackling tradition. Everyone was filled with an enthusiasm for his enterprise which carried all before it."

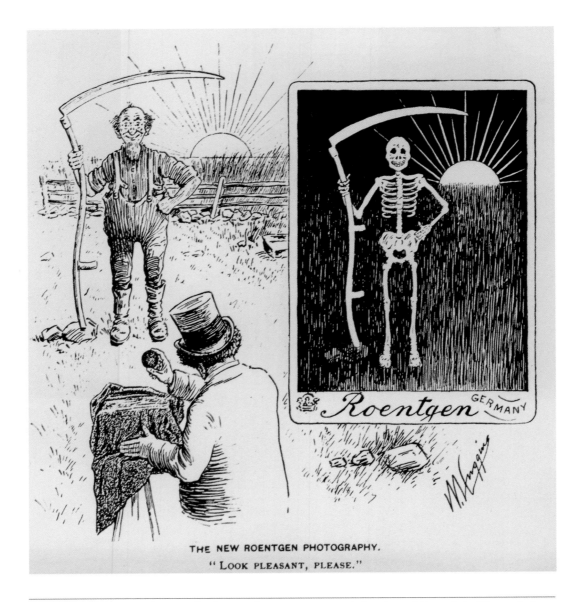

THE NEW ROENTGEN PHOTOGRAPHY.

"LOOK PLEASANT, PLEASE."

Above: The public's imagination regarding Roentgen's x-rays was captured almost as quickly as that of the medical community. Typical is this cartoon, which appeared in Life, February 1896, suggesting possibilities for the process well beyond diagnostics. Roentgen exhibitions became major attractions at public events, too. As the risks from random exposure were as yet unknown, curious civilians were invited to line up to have themselves and their loved ones "photographed."

Right: When physicist Wilhelm Konrad Roentgen, shown here, first discovered the form of light that he dubbed x-rays, he kept it a secret, secluding himself in his Würzburg University laboratory for seven weeks while he pondered its possibilities. He soon determined that the new technology would be useful as a means of illuminating broken and deformed bones and finding foreign objects lodged in tissue. But as the equipment improved, and he added film to the proceedings, he further discovered that it was possible to detect shadows of muscle and tissue as well. From there, it was but a short leap of the imagination to consider using radiography in the diagnosis of diseases, including diseases of the heart and circulation. Within a year of Roentgen's announcement in December 1895, more than 1,000 scientific papers, 50 books, and a journal, Archives of Clinical Skiagraphy *(shadow writing), appeared to document investigations. Roentgen is shown here eleven years after his momentous discovery, five years after receiving the first Nobel Prize for Physics.*

Aristotle had declared "the heart alone of all viscera cannot withstand injury," and as late as 1883, Vienna's renowned surgeon C.A. Theodor Billroth had agreed, saying "A surgeon who tries to suture a wound in the heart deserves to lose the esteem of his colleagues." Indeed, to so much as touch the working heart muscle was generally thought to cause it to stop beating, but Frankfurt surgeon Ludwig Rehn knew that this was not true of animal hearts, and he suspected that it was not true of human hearts either. Presented in 1896 with a young man who had received a stab wound to the anterior chest and who would clearly die without surgical intervention, Rehn decided to make the daring attempt. He opened the chest, found the pericardium distended with blood, and incised it widely so that he could see the life-threatening injury. As he suspected, the stab wound was actually small enough to stop with the pressure of a finger over the opening, but the leaking of blood would soon prove fatal if not stopped. Rehn determined to suture it closed, and he proceeded to take a series of single stitches with each split-second interval of diastole. As he had hoped, the sutures controlled the bleeding and the patient gradually recovered.

Daniel Hale Williams was the first African-American surgeon to attain distinction in heart surgery. A one-time cobbler's apprentice, river roustabout, and barber, Williams eventually graduated at age 27 from Chicago Medical College of Northwestern University in 1883. Opening a private practice in Chicago, he found himself excluded from the city's white-owned hospitals, so in 1891 he founded Provident Hospital as a facility cordial to all races. Two years later Williams made news again when he performed delicate surgery on a patient admitted with an arterial wound only a fraction of an inch from the heart itself and saved the man's life. Williams went on to found several medical associations offering membership to blacks and to work tirelessly on behalf of training generations of black doctors and nurses.

Blood-typing and blood compatibility were not understood as a prerequisite to safe human-to-human transfusions until the dawn of the 20th century, when antibody-antigen reactions were discovered as an aspect of the immune reaction. Using this information as a starting point, Karl Landsteiner, an assistant at the Institute of Pathological Anatomy in Vienna, studied blood samples of 22 subjects and concluded that the troublesome, sometimes deadly, transfusion reactions that occurred were the result of clumping of a donor's blood cells. He further traced the clumping to the presence of agglutinins in the recipient's serum, and based on the three distinct kinds of agglutinins he found, he designated them A, B, and C. Landsteiner, who is shown here in a photograph taken shortly after, went on to study the blood of scores of healthy individuals selected at random, ultimately leading to the modern designation of all human blood as belonging to either A, B, O, or AB types. By 1908, efforts were underway at the more advanced hospitals to select blood donors for surgical operations according to their compatibility. In 1911 Reuben Ottenberg, a researcher at Columbia University's biochemical laboratory, came up with a simple test to make matching easier and more reliable. Landsteiner himself turned to other challenges, isolating the poliomyelitis virus in 1908 and collaborating with others in discovering the Rh factor in blood in the 1940s. He received the Nobel Prize in Medicine or Physiology in 1930.

Infants born with congenital disorders of the heart had first been described on the basis of symptoms by a Danish physician in the 17th century. And in 1888 French physician Étienne-Louis Fallot had further defined the syndrome as stemming from a set of four congenital cardiac defects that came to be known as the tetralogy of Fallot. But it was Canadian-born Maude Abbott who truly laid the groundwork for the diagnosis and treatment of congenital heart defects. A protégée of William Osler, Abbott devoted her life to studying and classifying congenital heart disease as revealed in the postmortem examinations of more than 1,000 cases. She found the defects to consist of 24 distinct types. Though she met many obstacles to recognition in the male-dominated medical profession, her work was ultimately published in a monograph under the sponsorship of the American Heart Association in 1936, three years before she died.

Chapter Five

THE EMERGENCE OF CARDIOLOGY

*B*y the 20th century, there was little in terms of the gross anatomy and physiology of the heart that was not already known. But except for rare instances of surgical bravado, few physicians of the Victorian era were intellectually or technically prepared to do anything practical with the information. Enter cardiac specialization, modern developments in diagnostic equipment, and the rapid rise of surgical expertise, particularly in the United States.

The new century got off to a lively start in heart medicine in 1903 when Dutch physiologist Willem Einthoven adapted the string galvanometer, an instrument capable of measuring minute electric currents, to record the electrical activity of the human heart. Englishman Thomas Lewis was the first to grasp the enormous value of the electrocardiogram in detecting abnormal heart function; and in launching a journal devoted to its use, he did much to educate colleagues on both sides of the Atlantic.

Another major breakthrough at the turn of the century was in the area of reconstructing peripheral arteries. Many methods of splicing damaged veins and arteries had been tried previously. Mostly, they involved destructive ligation and obstruction of flow. (One gambit that enjoyed repeated attempts was the introduction of large masses of fine wire into an aneurysm, the idea being to stop the hemorrhaging via induced thrombosis, which was not entirely discarded until 1921.) Despite a few singular successes, none of the early procedures were considered even marginally reliable; indeed, many had disastrous consequences within hours of surgery.

Two Americans and a French émigré, working independently, tried radically different approaches to heart surgery, each with promising results. In 1896 John Benjamin Murphy of Northwestern University, succeeded in making the first of many end-to-end resections of damaged human arteries; his primary method was to trim the two broken ends, insert the smaller end into the larger for a short distance, and suture the splice closed. Six years later, legendary surgeon Rudolph Matas of Tulane University, New Orleans, developed a repair technique called "aneurysmorrhaphy," in which he managed to clean out an aneurysm, suture it internally, and restore arterial flow. And before the decade was over, in 1910 Frenchman Alexis Carrel of the Rockefeller Institute in New York devised still other solutions to the reconstruction puzzle, including triangulation suturing, closing an arterial hole with a venous patch and replacing an entire segment of damaged artery by means of a venous transplant. Carrel's technical accomplishments would bring him a Nobel Prize in 1912, but it would be another three decades before other surgeons felt confident enough to use his innovations as routine procedures.

Meanwhile, the same Ludwig Rehn who had performed direct surgery upon the heart in 1896 opened another major avenue of cardiovascular possibilities: in 1912 he performed the first resection of the pericardium in a procedure to treat constrictive pericarditis. Other truly pioneering work in the first half of this century included several surgical "firsts" in the United States. In 1923 Elliot Cutler of Boston repaired one of the serious complications of rheumatic fever, a calcified mitral valve in an 11-year-old girl; in 1938

Robert Gross, also of Boston, reconstructed one of the congenital defects of the great vessels, the patent ductus arteriosus; and Alfred Blalock at Johns Hopkins was the first to operate on a "blue baby" in 1943, an operation out of which came an infinite variety of other cardiac operations. By this time there were numbers of physicians and surgeons in the larger cities who comfortably called themselves specialists in the heart, with more choosing to concentrate on cardiology with each passing year.

At first, cardiac surgeons like Gross, Cutler, and Blalock had operated within the heart virtually by feel, as there was no way to keep the patient alive without a continuous flow of oxygenated blood to the brain. For more extensive and delicate procedures to be practicable, some sort of external pump was needed. After several aborted attempts and nearly two decades of exhaustive experimentation, Dr. John Gibbon, Jr., of Jefferson Medical College, Philadelphia, developed the first heart-lung machine and used it successfully in human heart surgery in 1953.

Six other indispensable "tools" in the modern cardiac surgeon's kit— anticoagulants, blood banks, fine suturing needles, penicillin, arteriography, and cardiac resuscitation techniques—all originated in the first half of the 20th century. Heparin, a natural anticoagulant substance found principally in the liver, was discovered in 1916 by Jay MacLean and William Howell of Johns Hopkins. A second anticoagulant was discovered in 1943: the slower-acting warfarin (coumarin). Both were forerunners of a series of chemical agents used in the management of platelet formation and, as such, important in cardio-vascular surgery. The first blood bank was established in 1937 at Chicago's Cook County Hospital; donor blood could now be drawn, typed, preserved without coagulating, and transfused into a patient on short notice. The first eyeless suturing needle was patented by a Massachusetts engineer in 1921; this made it possible to reduce by half the size of suturing holes, from which the leakage of blood in arteriovenous surgery had been a major problem.

The antibacterial action of penicillium mold was recognized by Sir Alexander Fleming in 1929, but it was employed as a "miracle drug" against infections, surgical and otherwise, only after World War II. And although arteriography traces its theoretical beginnings to Roentgen's x-ray machine, the practical use of imaging technology in the cardiac arena is more properly dated from 1911 with the development of the radio-kymograph, a kind of moving-picture x-ray that showed shadowy pictures of the heart beating second by second, and of the angiocardiogram, which was first used c. 1930. It was then that German surgeon Werner Forssmann performed the first cardiac catheterization, using himself as the experimental subject, and it became possible to see blockages and other heart anomalies in some detail.

Also aiding in the burgeoning of cardiology in these years was the support lent by private and public institutions. As a result of testing five million young men for military service in World War I, it had become apparent that the incidence of heart disease in the American population was sufficient to be a matter of public health concern. In 1924 the American Heart Association was founded as a national organization of public health physicians dedicated to identifying and preventing the leading causes of heart disease. Private foundations like the Rockefeller Institute, founded in 1901, invested substantial sums to support individual pathologists and physiologists in cardiovascular research. And the federal government, spurred by the successful example of such public health campaigns as the tuberculosis and polio drives, not to mention the effectiveness of World War II programs like its own Manhattan Project, decided to put its financial muscle into heart research. By the late 1940s, cardiology was on the verge of a Golden Age.

Dutchman Willem Einthoven poses in his laboratory alongside his original string galvanometer, which was introduced in 1903. This device, the first electrocardiograph, made it possible to record the heart's electrical activity, an ideal means to evaluate disorders of heartbeat, or arrhythmias. Shown under the right-hand photo is a sample tracing from an early instrument. Such records not only provided direct information from the heart, but they could be filed away for later study and comparison. Einthoven, a professor of physiology at Leiden, got his idea for the string galvanometer from the earlier galvanometers of French physiologist Jacques Arsène d'Arsonval, but instead of the original coiled wire through which electrical currents were conducted, Einthoven hit on the idea of using very fine quartz fibers and coating the infinitely finer string produced with silver to make a more sensitive lightweight conductor. He also devised the means to magnify the string's motion some 660 times through the addition of a magnifying lens and to project this image on a special recording camera. Time marking was obtained by the simultaneous projection of the shadows cast by the spokes of a rotating bicycle wheel, which was turned by a constant-speed electric motor. To facilitate patient exams in the hospital, an arrangement was initially made to send the graphed images via telephone wires to the laboratory nearly a mile away for recording and interpretation.

One of Einthoven's subjects is shown being tested with a 1911 table model of the electrocardiograph. The subject sits with both arms and a leg immersed in large pails of saline solution, an arrangement that facilitated conduction. This later model represents a considerable downscaling of the original instrument, whose battery of equipment filled two rooms and took five people to run. It was manufactured by Cambridge Scientific Instrument Company, which was the only manufacturer licensed to produce his device in the early years. Einthoven's invention inaugurated a whole new specialty within cardiology and earned him the Nobel Prize in Medicine or Physiology in 1924.

British clinical physiologist Thomas Lewis acquired the first commercially made electrocardiograph for University College Hospital, London, in 1909. In doing so, he was the first among the English-speaking medical community to become adept at its use. Over the next decade it was largely through the findings issuing from Lewis' laboratory—some 100 papers all told—that the value of this tool came to be understood by American practitioners. Lewis was also the motive force behind the journal Heart. The journal, begun in 1909, holds the distinction of being the first professional publication devoted to the specialty of cardiovascular research.

James Mackenzie, of London Hospital, was regarded by colleagues on both sides of the Atlantic as the preeminent authority on the heart in the early decades of the 20th century. His studies included books on the pulse (1902), on heart disease (1908), on symptomatic diagnosis (1909), and on angina pectoris (1923), a disease of which he would die in 1925. Mackenzie also developed the ink polygraph and was the first to systematically investigate multiform arrhythmias. He is also remembered as the modern figure who reintroduced digitalis as a treatment for certain heart conditions. Indeed, it was Mackenzie's recommendation in Diseases of the Heart *that prompted Teddy Roosevelt's personal physician to put the ailing ex-president on a regimen of digitalis in the months shortly before his death. Unfortunately, the recommendation came too late to reverse Roosevelt's health problems.*

Louis Bishop was perhaps the first practitioner to specialize in cardiology by design. (Though James Mackenzie was regarded by others as a heart specialist, he had always sought to deny it, preferring to think of himself as a clinician of broader skills.) Trained as an internist, Bishop entered private practice in 1892 after obtaining first-class medical training at the College of Physicians and Surgeons of New York and completing a two-year internship at St. Luke's Hospital. Within a few years he had chosen to concentrate on "diseases of the chest," and by 1907 he carried the title of "clinical professor of diseases of the heart and circulation" at Fordham University, from which position he was able to devote himself to cardiologic matters entirely. Bishop worked in an era of tremendous change for medicine. As a contemporary commented with only a little exaggeration, it was risky for any serious diagnostician to sleep more than eight or nine hours without running the risk of becoming a Rip Van Winkle character, totally out of phase with developments. Bishop seems to have done a good job of keeping up.

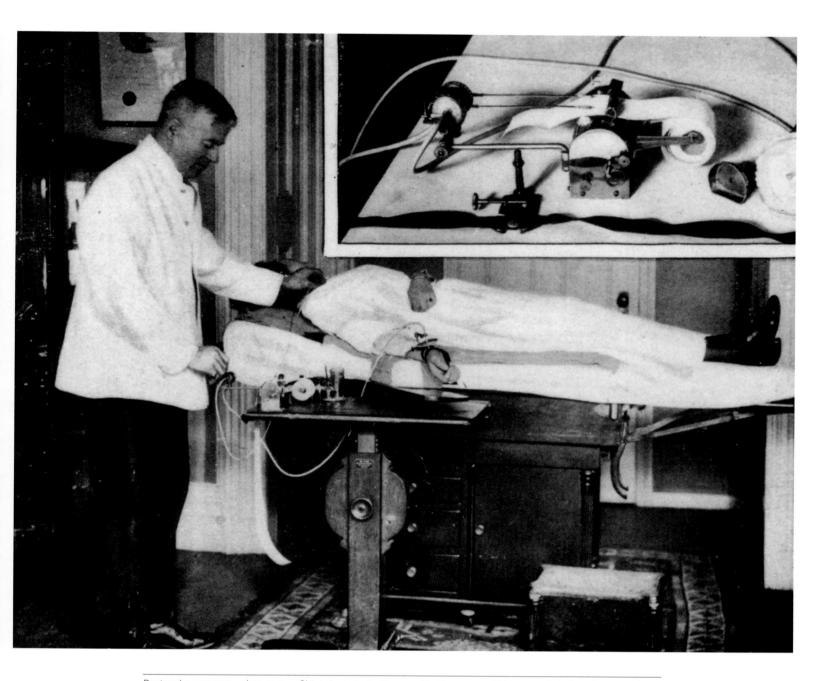

During the summers, when many of his private patients moved to the country, Bishop traveled abroad to study heart treatments. In particular, he made repeated trips to Bad Nauheim, a world center in cardiologic care. At Bad Nauheim, Bishop observed the mix of advanced technological fare—x-rays and electrocardiograms—incorporating many of these procedures into his own practice, as reported in his book Heart Troubles, Their Prevention and Relief, published in 1921. Shown above is Dr. Bishop as he records pulse tracings using the Mackenzie polygraph c. 1920. Bishop also prescribed various low-tech treatments, especially the so-called "Nauheim regimen." Developed by Nauheim physician Theodor Schott, it combined carbonated baths with special diet and resistive exercises.

In the first decades of the 20th century, there was considerable disparity in the variety of medical diagnostic technology to be found in the practitioner's office. Dr. Alexander Barkley, who called himself an internist and practiced in Oklahoma in those years, pioneered the use of x-rays to assess some conditions as the above photo (1916) records. The more typical physician still made do with somewhat less. In the (recreated) suburban Philadelphia office of Dr. Philip Gordon Kitchen (left), conveniences include an adjustable examining table, a telephone, weighing scales, a sphygmomanometer, and electricity. However, Kitchen still lacked such niceties as running water.

Chicago's Presbyterian Hospital, later Rush-Presbyterian Hospital, installed its first electrocardiogram c. 1913. By this time, the relevant machinery had become somewhat less elaborate and more suitable for clinical use. It was, however, still very costly. The price of this instrument was the rough equivalent of $20,000 in current U.S. dollars.

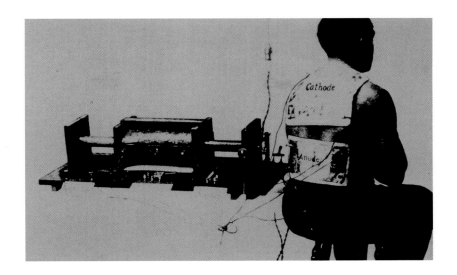

A device designed to deliver rhythmic electrostimulation to hearts in cardiac arrest was an idea developed by Louise Robinovitch, a medical researcher on staff at St-Anne Asylum Hospital in Paris. Writing about the invention (shown here in two views) in the Journal of Mental Pathology, 1909, Robinovitch reports that she was prompted to the idea by intervening in a situation at her hospital. A young female morphine addict was being examined when she "had a sudden attack of syncope. Various means were used to revive her, and she regained consciousness...then fell into a second attack; her respirations became slow, shallow, appearing at very rare intervals—perhaps four or five per minute; the pulse was almost imperceptible, and her face was blue—almost black-blue—from asphyxia." Robinovitch stated that various methods of artificial respiration were tried for 20 minutes, to no effect, after which Robinovitch volunteered to bring her "special coil for resuscitation" which she was experimenting with elsewhere in the hospital and see if it had any effect. After attaching the cathodes, one in the dorsal region, the other in the lumbar region, she "practiced rhythmic excitations during a period of about 30 seconds...It was astonishing to see the accompanying change of color in the patient's face." After two more excitations, "the patient took a long spontaneous breath, and opened her eyes." Robinovitch concluded with the suggestion that such an instrument be carried on ambulances in order to treat patients en route to the hospital. Although she continued to work on her idea, the equipment (above), no practical application was adopted by hospitals for many years.

The long march toward developing artificial pacemakers had many participants and a history of experimentation spread over more than half a century. An early U.S. contributor to progress was Joseph Erlanger of Washington University, St. Louis, who is shown here in 1905. Erlanger studied the physiology of heart blockage in dogs and demonstrated that it was possible to alter heart rate and rhythm by exciting the sinoatrial node (the natural "pacemaker") by electrical stimulation with a transthoracic electrode. Erlanger, together with his collaborator Herbert Glasser at the Rockefeller Institute, was awarded the Nobel Prize for Medicine or Physiology in 1944, when they were cited for research on the functions of single nerve fibers and their discovery that various types of nerve fibers conduct impulses at various speeds.

James B. Herrick is remembered for his classic essay on coronary thrombosis, "Clinical Features of Sudden Obstruction of the Coronary Arteries," published in a 1912 issue of the Journal of the American Medical Association. Herrick, a professor of medicine at Rush Medical College, devoted much of his career to the public health aspects of heart disease prevention. He was a leader in establishing the Chicago Association for the Prevention and Relief of Heart Disease, which was formed in 1922. As in other cities, the primary efforts of the Chicago group of heart specialists were in diagnosing and treating "public patients" through low-cost heart clinics. In this endeavor, they ran afoul of family physicians who resented what appeared to be encroachment on their professional territory. Herrick later served two terms as president of the American Heart Association.

Lewis Conner, a professor of medicine at Cornell-New York Hospital, was a founder and first president of the American Heart Association. The group, which was born out of discussions held at an annual meeting of the American Medical Association in 1922, took as its model the public health objectives of the anti-tuberculosis movement. Its goals were to develop research, collect and distribute statistical data bearing on the incidence of heart disease, improve patient access to specialized medical services, and make the public, including family physicians, generally more conscious of the extent of the heart disease problem. After two more years of planning, the AHA was formally organized in 1924. Its initial leadership was entirely made up of physicians, and all but two members had academic affiliations with a strong bent toward the public health aspects of cardiac research and treatment. A year later, the AHA launched the bimonthly American Heart Journal. Together, the AHA and the Journal played a key role in the next two decades in defining the parameters of cardiac specialization.

One of the outstanding researchers in early 20th century heart surgery was the controversial but brilliant Frenchman Alexis Carrel. Carrel came to the United States in 1903, believing his chances for the free expression of his medical curiosity were greater in the more liberal investigative atmosphere to be found there. After a brief stint in Chicago, Carrel was invited to join the Rockefeller Institute for Medical Research in New York, the first American institution devoted wholly to medical research. The choice proved to be good for both, and during his tenure Carrel carried out scores of remarkable experiments in vascular surgery, many of which would not be repeated by other surgeons for another 30 years. Carrel won the Nobel Prize for Medicine in 1912 "in recognition of his work on vascular suture, the transplantation of blood vessels and organs." Carrel is shown here (at center in his French-style uniform) with a group of young surgeons in 1917, when Carrel was lent by the Rockefeller Institute to the U.S. Army to train men in wartime surgical techniques.

The first documented human cardiac catheterization was performed by Werner Forssmann in Eberswald, Germany, in 1928. Inserting what Forssmann described as a "well-oiled ureteral catheter" into the antecubital vein of his own arm, he maneuvered the probe all the way—about 65 cm—to the right atrium. He then "examined the position of the catheter by means of a mirror which was held by a nurse in front of a fluoroscopic screen" and took an image. Forssmann continued his investigations over the next two years, seeking suitable radiopaque materials to inject into the heart as a means of better visualizing its chambers. Once again, he used himself as investigative subject and found that the "heart probe" he sought was eminently possible. Regarded with suspicion by the medical establishment, Forssmann was unable to obtain any further hospital appointments in suitable research hospitals in Germany. Discouraged, he abandoned his work to become a small-town general practitioner. His originality and personal heroism did not go unnoticed abroad, however, and in 1956, around the time this photo was taken he was given the Nobel Prize for Medicine.

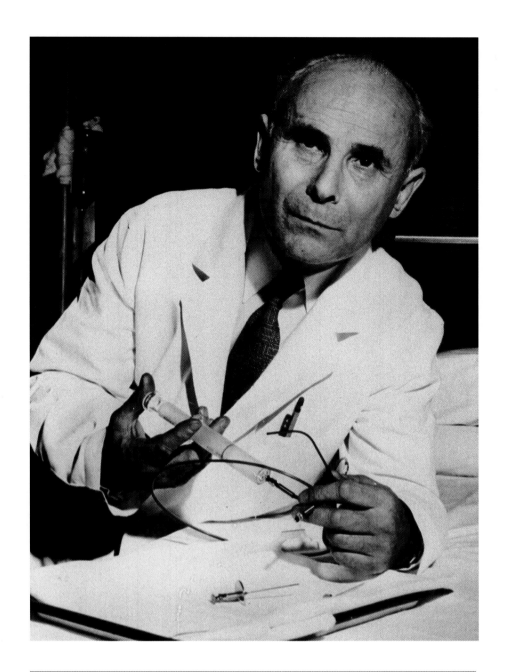

Physiologist André Cournand, M.D., (above) was a corecipient of Forssmann's 1956 Nobel Prize along with Bellevue Hospital colleague Dickinson Richards, M.D. Cournand and Richards had continued Forssmann's work, performing detailed, quantitative physiological studies of the heart through intracardiac catheterization. Once the profession recognized the procedure's value, it rapidly became a standard tool in the diagnosis and treatment of heart disease, and soon virtually every advanced medical center boasted at least one team of cardiac interventionists.

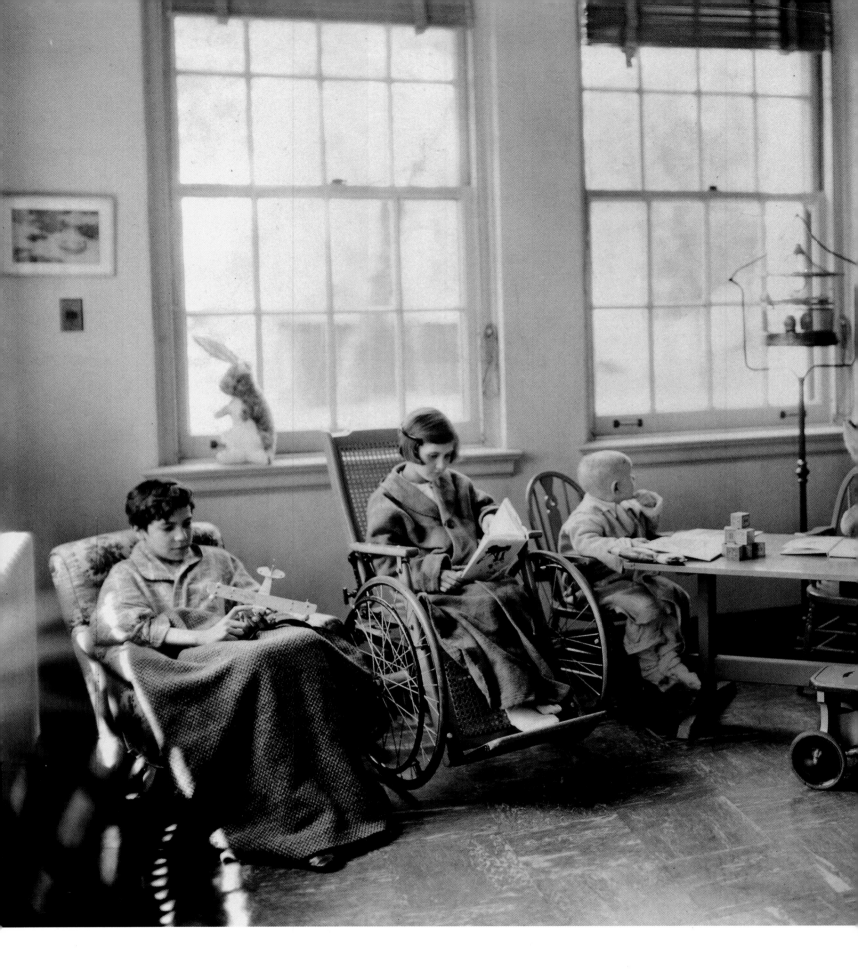

Rheumatic fever was a prevalent cause of cardiac disease before the era of antibiotics. Because the fever occurs in the aftermath of a streptococcal infection, such as strep throat, its victims were most likely to be young children. The damage, which was often irreversible, involved serious injuries to the endocardium, the pericardium, or the heart muscle and its valves. Here, a group of children recuperate at Children's Hospital, Minneapolis, Minnesota, in 1932. Many youngsters remained in facilities like these for years, their long-term treatment consisting of bed rest, sunshine, physical therapy, and nutritious food.

A young rheumatic fever patient at Massachusetts General Hospital enjoys the full attention of several eminent cardiologists in this 1925 photo. Among those assembled at left are Howard Sprague and T. Duckett Jones. Paul Dudley White (above), who had received specialized cardiology training under Thomas Lewis and James Mackenzie in London, was Mass General's first staff cardiologist. In this position, which he occupied from 1920 to 1960, he became America's best-known heart specialist, carrying out cardiac research and training more than 200 resident physicians, among them Sprague and Jones. White went on to gain recognition as a frequent participant on government health committees. When President Dwight D. Eisenhower suffered a heart attack in 1955, White became his high-profile cardiologist.

The late 1920s saw the beginnings of a new fitness fad that reached all the way to the president's residence and its occupant, Herbert Hoover. A cross between tennis and volleyball was adapted for early morning play each day on the White House lawn as a means of keeping Hoover, his cabinet, and staffers in trim. "Hoover Ball," as it came to be known, was supposedly developed by Hoover's Navy physician, Joel Boone, M.D. when he became concerned about Hoover's expanding waistline. Under the rules of Boone's game, teams of two to four players batted a six-pound medicine ball back and forth. "Stopping a six-pound ball with steam back of it, returning it with similar steam, is not pink-tea stuff," wrote a correspondent covering the sport for the New York Times. "Dr. Boone estimates that as much beneficial exercise is obtained from half an hour of it as from three times as much tennis or six times as much golf." Only once did Hoover reportedly skip his cardiovascular workout; otherwise, he reported for duty six days a week, rain or shine, for four years, from 7 AM to 7:30 AM sharp, an admirable record by any standard.

At a laboratory in Paris c. 1930, researchers monitor a group of recording devices as a man pushes a wheelbarrow up a slight incline to demonstrate a primitive version of the modern stress test. The subject wears a mask that collects expired air into an analysis jar, presumably to monitor oxygen/CO_2 levels. At the same time, lines attached to arm and wrist cuffs gather information on the participant's blood pressure and pulse.

The first out-of-body "artificial heart" made its debut in 1936, the result of teamwork between Rockefeller Institute's Alexis Carrel and aviation pioneer Charles Lindbergh. Both men had become interested in the notion of finding a way to divert natural circulation long enough to perform necessary surgery on the organ and its major arteries. Lindbergh hoped to help a relative whose heart condition, he had been told, was beyond repair; Carrel saw the device as crucial to basic research. Introduced by a mutual acquaintance in 1930, they began work soon after. Over the next five years, Lindbergh produced a half dozen versions of the perfusion pump that would bear his name, the work being interrupted only briefly when his son was kidnapped and murdered. At the pump's unveiling, Carrel predicted that it would soon be possible that "organs removed from the human body in the course of an operation, or soon after death, could be revived," adding that it would also be possible to remove diseased organs from the body in order to treat them more aggressively, sustaining patients with the pump until their own organs could be cured and replanted.

Lindbergh's final version of the perfusion pump stood two feet tall and was designed to hold the heart of a freshly killed animal—usually a cat or a chicken that had been bled to death—in the large diagonal main chamber. A glass tube was then fitted to the main artery of the heart and the chamber sealed. The entire device was attached to a sophisticated pump whose valve rotated in precise imitation of the systolic and diastolic pressures of the natural beating heart, as it allowed gas to flow into the glass apparatus much as it would flow naturally into the arteries. The gas, in turn, pushed artificial blood up from the base of the machine into the organ. Gravity then permitted the fluid to drain out again into a chamber for recycling. The artificial blood used was a mix of the animal's own blood and additives devised by Carrel's assistants. Coincident with Lindbergh's work on the pump, he also devised a centrifuge that simultaneously separated blood plasma from serum and washed the cells.

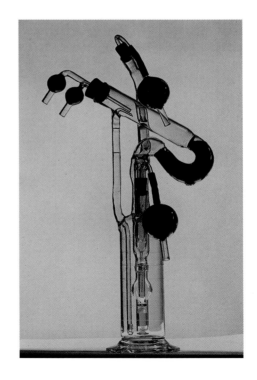

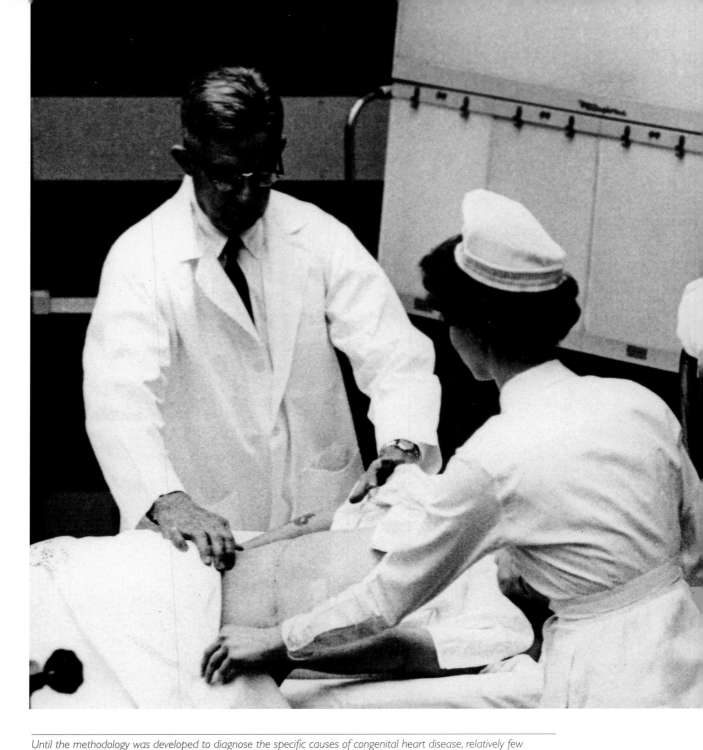

Until the methodology was developed to diagnose the specific causes of congenital heart disease, relatively few advances were made in the surgical techniques needed to correct them. The first sorties in this specialized area had been made by Maude Abbott at the turn of the century when she classified congenital malfunctions on the basis of postmortem examinations. The next leap forward is credited to Helen Taussig, a pediatric cardiologist at Johns Hopkins, top right. In the 1930s Taussig developed the classic techniques for identifying various types of congenital disorders on the basis of fluoroscopic and ECG readings of living patients with abnormal hearts. She then turned her attention to assisting "blue babies," those infants whose skin was continuously bluish or cyanotic rather than the usual healthy pink. Their problem was most often that blood was not becoming sufficiently oxygenated due to a hole in the partition separating the left and right ventricles. Taussig needed to find a surgeon who dared to sew a branch of the baby's aorta into a pulmonary artery to recirculate blood through the lungs. She found the surgeon in Alfred Blalock, who came to Hopkins in 1941 and performed the first "blue baby shunt" in 1943. Blalock went on to develop numbers of other cardiac shunt operations and to train scores of cardiac surgeons; he is shown here at a patient's bedside as he conducts one of his fourth-year surgical clinics. Blalock is also remembered for his pioneering work on the relationship between surgical shock and decreased blood circulation. The two pioneers are also shown, bottom right at a ceremony honoring their work.

During World War II, President Franklin D. Roosevelt asked Vannevar Bush, Director of the Office of Scientific Research and Development, to draw up a proposal for a federal initiative in medical research. In due course, a number of programs evolved that would ultimately give major stimulus to academic cardiology and transform the practice of medical care in diseases of the heart and circulatory system. Among the landmark events contributing to these changes in the late 1940s were the enactment by Congress of the National Heart Act, the foundation of the National Heart Institute (forerunner of the NIH's National Heart, Lung, and Blood Institute), and the formation of the National Health Advisory Council. This last group, shown in the 1949 photograph on this page, included executive director Paul Dudley White, medical research philanthropist Mary Lasker, and noted surgeon Michael DeBakey. Coincident with the federal government's plunge into heart research, the American Heart Association began to transform itself from a physician-centered operation into a voluntary health organization in 1948. Its avowed purpose was to raise the awareness of ordinary citizens as well as that of elected officials of the public health crisis in heart disease. With this change of direction at the AHA, the way was open for a group of physicians specializing in cardiological practice to form the American College of Cardiology to meet their professional needs. The ACC's first president, Franz Groedel, who emigrated from Germany to the United States in 1933, became one of the founding members.

Discovered in 1928 by Scottish bacteriologist Sir Alexander Fleming, penicillin had been developed under a crash program within the U.S. drug industry for military use during World War II. The antibiotic had saved tens of thousands of lives from battlefield infections but remained in short supply until 1945, when it began to be available for civilian medical purposes. Other antibiotics followed, including streptomycin and the first of the tetracyclines. Penicillin, in particular, changed the practice of cardiology because it greatly reduced the risks of streptococcal infections, the underlying cause of rheumatic fever and bacterial endocarditis. As a broad-spectrum antibiotic, it also opened the way for more extensive surgical explorations of the heart.

The Framingham Heart Study was undertaken in 1948 under a grant from the National Institutes of Health/National Heart, Lung, and Blood Institute. It pioneered the concept that a collection of undetermined risk factors was somehow associated with the incidence of stroke and heart disease in the general population. Organizers started with 5,127 healthy men and women between the ages of 30 and 60—roughly every other adult in Framingham, Massachusetts—and followed developments in each person's health over a period of many years, hoping to learn which individuals with what kinds of genetic and lifestyle patterns developed disease. Subjects were interviewed and tested biannually, a procedure shown in these photos from the 1950s. As time went on, children of some of the original subjects were also brought into the study. After several decades, two different statistical groups emerged within the larger study: those who had suffered stroke or heart attack and those who had not—yet. And with these distinctions a picture—really, more of a set of common risk factors such as smoking, elevated body-mass index, high blood pressure, high cholesterol levels, sedentary lifestyle, and excess emotional stress—began to emerge. As the data accumulated, government and private organizations have waged increasingly vigorous campaigns to make people more aware of their own susceptibility to heart disease and the preventive measures they can take to improve their odds.

The tempo of discoveries and new technologies speeded up notably in the 1940s and 1950s.
Dwight Harken of Harvard (shown center) and Charles Bailey of Hahnemann, capitalizing on
wartime experiences treating battlefield wounds, especially shell fragments embedded around
the heart, simultaneously developed bold new approaches to dealing with mitral stenosis. In 1948
both surgeons operated on patients with severely deformed mitral valves, inserting fingers through
incisions into the left atrial while the hearts continued to pump blood. Though several of their first
patients died, the successes encouraged them to persevere. Another important step was taken
in 1951, when Charles Hufnagel (above) of Georgetown University, Washington DC, developed a
prosthetic plastic valve replacement to treat aortic insufficiency as well as the surgical technique
to implant it. In 1952, F. John Lewis of the University of Minnesota went another step toward open
heart surgery when he closed an atrial septal defect in a five-year-old patient. To achieve a blood-
less field in which to operate, Lewis blocked the return of blood to the heart for more than five
minutes, protecting the affected organs by temporarily lowering body temperature to 79°F. What
was needed for more complicated surgical procedures was a device that could keep oxygenated
blood flowing everywhere else in the body while the heart was stopped so that the surgeon could
enjoy a clear vision of the area he was working in. This need was met when John H. Gibbon, Jr. (left)
of the Jefferson Medical College, Philadelphia, introduced the first external heart-lung machine.

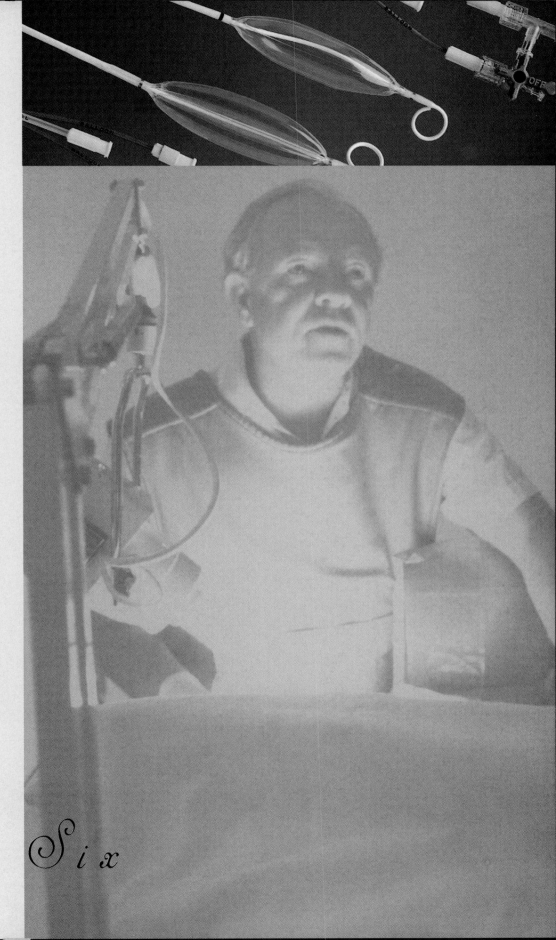

Chapter Six

THE FINAL FRONTIERS

In an effort to forecast educational needs for America's future doctors, the Association of American Medical Colleges published a report in 1965 on current trends in health care. Among the major forces shaping medicine, and cardiology in particular, were increasing demands for specialization among physicians and surgeons, stunning advances in scientific knowledge, and a growing dependence on sophisticated medical technology. Also cited were the nation's aging population, the emergence of the hospital as the locus of cardiac health care, the growth of health insurance, and expanding government involvement in all aspects of medical research and treatment. Not mentioned, but certainly a factor in the rising demand for cardiac care, was the high rate of heart disease. Long the leading cause of death in the United States, the incidence of congenital and acquired disorders associated with the heart and circulatory system had actually been rising since the 1920s, despite medicine's improving ability to treat them. As was becoming increasingly apparent, changes in the U.S. lifestyle and diet were at least partially to blame for this distressing record. A stepped-up public health campaign was also needed— and quickly.

As it has turned out, the last decades of the 20th century have brought enormous progress to many aspects of cardiovascular treatment and preventive care. In diagnosis, a battery of sophisticated equipment has been developed to identify and monitor various types of heart disease. First came electrocardiography, based on ultrasound, as a noninvasive tool for imaging intracardiac structures. Following the work of pioneers in the late 1950s in Sweden, cardiologists like

Claude Joyner of the University of Pennsylvania and Harvey Feigenbaum of Indiana University, used the system to diagnose mitral valve stenosis, pericardial effusion, and atrial thrombus.

The first selective coronary arteriography was performed in 1958 by F. Mason Sones, Jr., a cardiologist at the Cleveland Clinic. Nonselective coronary arteriography had been a known technique since the late 1940s, but it had never been entirely satisfactory because the images it provided of coronary arteries were rarely of good quality. By using a catheter to selectively inject contrast material solely in the coronary arteries, Sones' newer method promised much better resolution than anything previously known. The technology only got better when, six years later, cardiac radiologist Melvin Judkins at the University of Oregon developed a series of soft catheters preshaped to fit the anatomical channels they traveled down. Radiocardiography, the earliest of the nuclear imaging technologies, had made it possible, beginning in 1949, to measure coronary blood flow under a variety of conditions, including stress, and to detect acute myocardial infarction. It has since been largely supplanted by three-dimensional computed x-ray tomography (PET and SPECT technologies) and magnetic resonance imaging, each of which has specialized diagnostic uses in imaging the cardiovascular system.

The artificial pacemaker came into wide use in this era, providing life-saving support to huge numbers of people who would otherwise live in fear of sudden, fatal arrhythmia. The first instruments were bulky external instruments that kept their users plugged into a major electrical source. But with the development of transistors and miniaturized batteries, these wondrous devices eventually became suitable for permanent implantation. Biosensors (added still later) make them able to adjust their output to respond to changes in adrenaline, oxygen, and other chemicals for still more refined levels of control.

The most dramatic of surgical events have unquestionably revolved around heart transplantation and the artificial heart, which were first tried in the 1960s. But in terms of the frequency with which it is used and the numbers of lives affected, coronary artery bypass graft surgery (CABGS) was the most important breakthrough of recent years. The first account of CABGS was published in 1968 by René Favaloro of the Cleveland Clinic. He described treating angina pectoris by means of a radical method of bypassing the obstruction: it involved grafting a section of leg vein between the aorta and a diseased coronary artery to provide a new channel for blood flow. Favaloro's proposal initially met with considerable doubt, not to mention harsh criticism in some quarters, but within a rather short time, its value was confirmed. By 1972, there were some 20,000 such operations being performed annually; five years later the number was closer to 70,000. Its numbers have continued to climb, with 600,000 bypass surgeries anticipated for 1998.

Another procedure, known as balloon angioplasty, appeared as a safer, less intrusive, and less expensive alternative for many kinds of angina in 1964. An outgrowth of diagnostic catheterization, it was born almost by chance when Charles Dotter, a vascular radiologist at the University of Oregon, noted that sometimes when he withdrew the conventional catheter used in probing a patient's occluded artery, it left an open channel behind. He began to experiment with the idea of using a catheter tip to remodel the inside of clogged arteries by design. Dotter's ideas were slow to be accepted, but over the next 15 years, others began to experiment, especially in the design of catheter tips, with the procedure eventually gaining a wide following. Today, balloon angioplasty accounts for more than 400,000 surgical procedures annually.

With so much going on in the arena of heart disease, hospitals made adjustments to the way they managed heart patients. Notably, in the 1960s the larger hospitals introduced cardiac care units where the sickest heart patients could be monitored 24 hours a day by specially trained staff with immediate access to the most advanced equipment. Outpatient departments developed prevention and rehabilitation programs to help patients at risk of coronary disease live better and longer.

Cardiopulmonary resuscitation also became a skill widely practiced not only by trained physicians and technicians in hospitals but by countless ordinary citizens who learned the simple techniques through their local Red Cross or fire department.

As the century comes to a close, the outlook for heart patients has never been brighter. Much that was mysterious about the heart even two or three decades ago is now understood with remarkable clarity. Medical research has found convincing evidence of the roles played by diet, exercise, stress, and smoking. An array of remarkable cardiovascular drugs has also been developed to treat many once-intractable conditions; some are even able to interrupt a heart attack in progress. And before the year 2000, we will almost certainly see the first fruits of gene therapy in cardiology. Perhaps the largest hurdle ahead now is in our willingness to take better care of the hearts we have.

The first wearable, external, battery-powered heart pacemaker had its beginnings in 1949 in this modest garage in Minneapolis, Minnesota. Here, Earl Bakken, a graduate student in electrical engineering, and his friend Palmer Hermundslie set up shop to repair and modify medical equipment for the doctors and medical researchers at Northwestern Hospital. In time, the enterprise, known as Medtronic, entered into a collaboration with C. Walton Lillehei, a pioneer heart surgeon. Lillehei needed a device to aid patients recovering from corrective open heart procedures—something that would keep the heart beating at an acceptable rate until it could run smoothly on its own. (As early as 1932, Albert Hyman of New York had demonstrated the feasibility of pacing the heart with a pulse of electricity, but Hyman's mode of delivery via a needle electrode through the chest wall was impractical, as were several other interim developments.) Together, Lillehei and Bakken devised a pacemaker system that would be less bulky, fully portable, and more reliable than the earlier devices that worked only when the patient was stationary and literally "plugged in" to an electrical outlet. One major key to their success was the invention in 1948 of the semiconductor transistor, which made possible the gradual miniaturization of the mechanisms needed to run pacemakers.

Right: Dr. C. Walton Lillehei of the University of Minnesota Medical School pioneered cardiac pacing for young patients, the repair of whose congenital heart defects was his specialty. Here, Lillehei examines a youngster wearing one of the first external pacemakers. In the years before the development of the heart-lung machine, Lillehei was also an innovator in a procedure known as "controlled cross-circulation," in which a blood-compatible human "donor"—often a parent—was temporarily connected to a young patient undergoing open-heart surgery, and the donor's heart and lungs were used to oxygenate the blood. The method was, by any measure, a risky procedure that was reserved for situations where all other options had been exhausted. It was discontinued soon after being introduced.

Below: Medtronic's first pacemaker unit, developed in 1957 and shown here, was about the size of a paperback book. The circuitry to run it was patterned after a transistorized metronome Earl Bakken had seen, and the pacemaker's power came from mercury batteries that delivered a 9-volt DC pulse. The whole rig was compact enough to be worn even by young patients and the frail elderly. The next significant development in pacing was the Chardack-Greatbatch pacemaker implant, which was developed by Dr. William Chardack and Wilson Greatbatch, an electrical engineer. Their "permanent" device, the result of two years of collaboration and experimentation, became available in 1960. In its earliest form, the Chardack-Greatbatch pacemaker implant measured roughly 65 mm in diameter, was 15 mm thick, and included 10 long-life, replaceable battery cells. The device cost patients $375 and was designed to be worn for years rather than months.

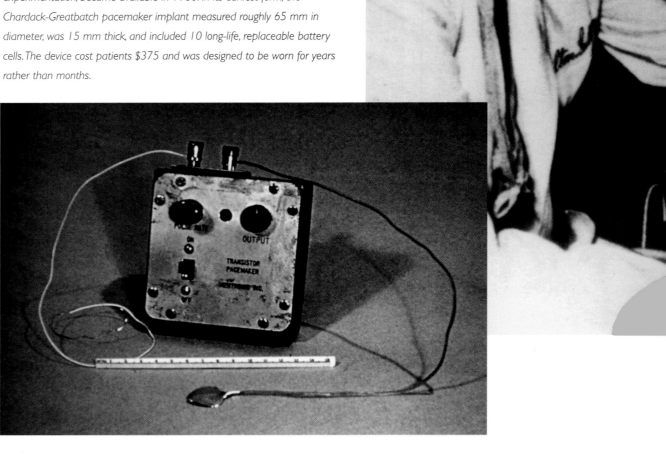

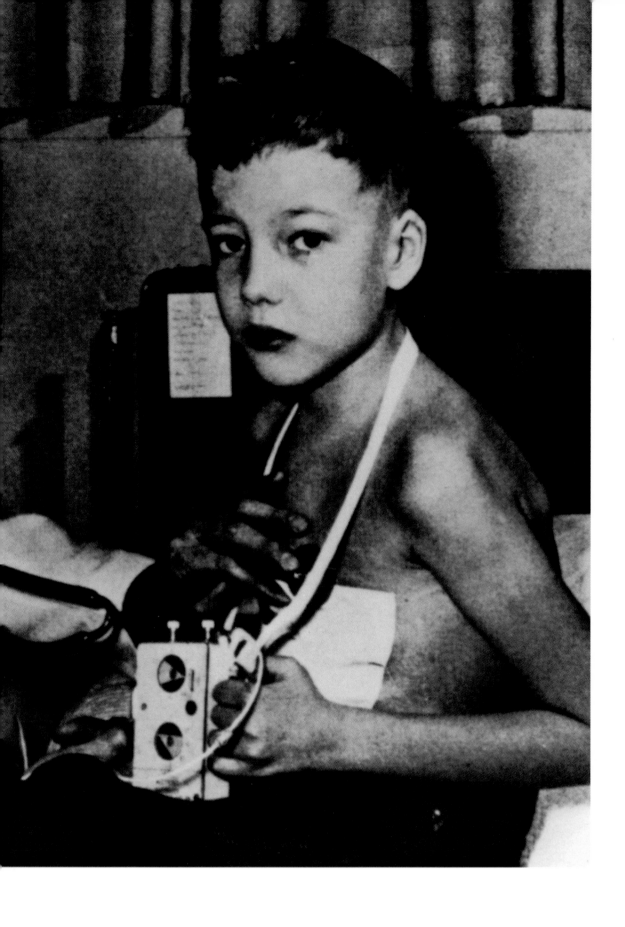

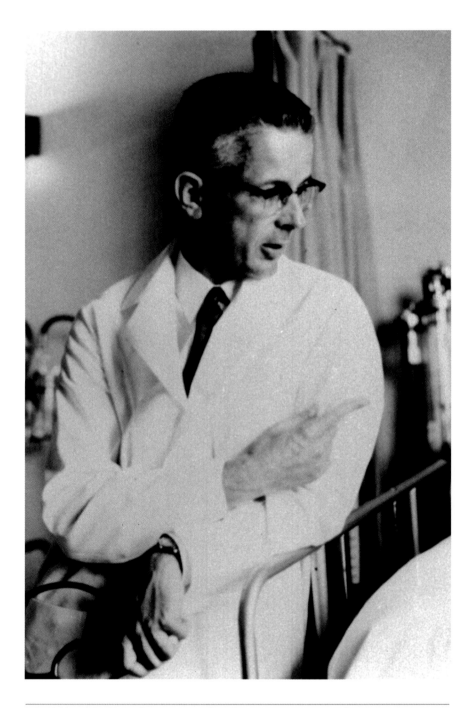

John Kirklin of the Mayo Clinic was one of the first surgeons to use the Gibbon-type heart-lung machine (right), despite a 50% mortality rate experienced in the early years. Kirklin is shown above in a photo taken in 1967 as he makes a postop visit with one of his patients.

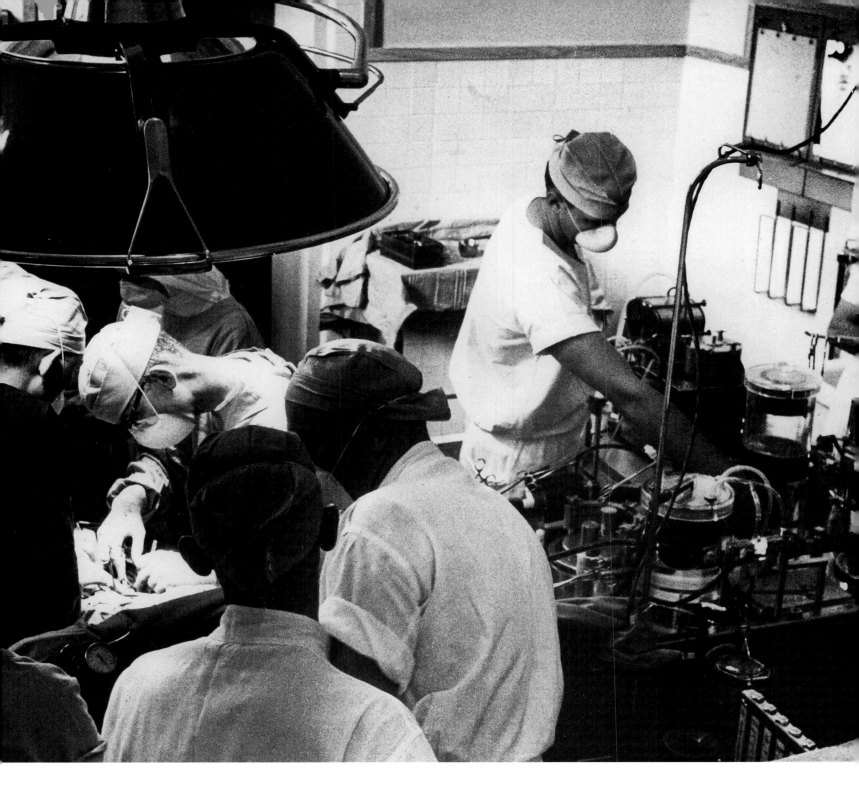

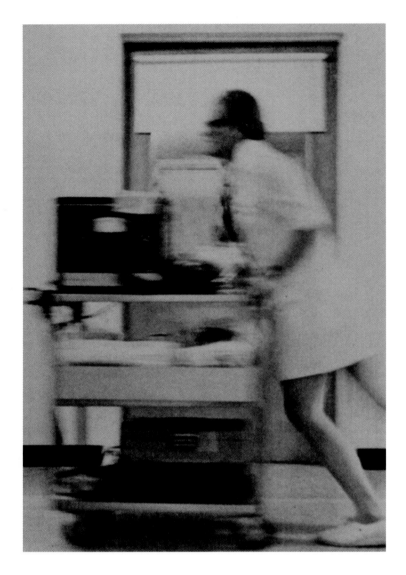

Cardiologist Hughes Day of Kansas City introduced the concept of the coronary care unit to U.S. hospitals in 1961. Day, who came to this notion virtually at the same moment that Desmond Julian was experimenting with it in Edinburgh, Scotland, persuaded the management of Bethany Medical Center that the CCU could provide superior care and monitoring, particularly for those patients who had suffered myocardial infarction and were at acute risk of further stoppages. As he pointed out, a particular advantage of the centralized unit was that it put vulnerable patients within easy reach of the defibrillator, which in these early years was a huge, ungainly machine that could be moved to the bedside only with great difficulty. And subsequent experience in a number of hospitals that tried the concept showed that admission to such units conferred a significant survival advantage over care administered in the standard hospital room. Between 1961 and 1972, more than 2,300 CCUs had been opened nationwide. The typical unit contained beds for five to ten patients, with a ratio of specially trained nurses and other personnel to patients of at least one to two. It was equipped with monitoring equipment that provided a continuous, often audible, record of each patient's heart rhythm, respiratory rate, and other key indicators. Closely related to the CCU concept was another idea that came out of Kansas City: the portable cardiac resuscitation unit on wheels, or "crash cart" (left). While no match for the CCU, the crash cart has become standard equipment in emergency rooms and on the intensive care wards of smaller hospitals.

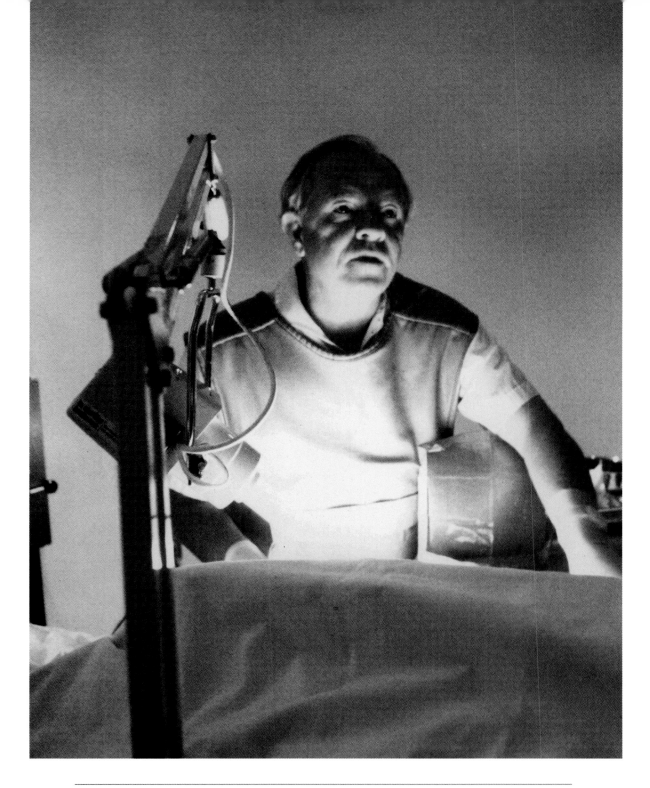

F. Mason Sones, Jr., a pediatric cardiologist at the Cleveland Clinic in Cleveland, Ohio, is credited with having invented selective coronary angiography. Sones stumbled on the discovery in 1958 as he performed an angiogram on a 26-year-old man with rheumatic heart disease. While preparing to inject a contrast dye into the aortic valve to assess the severity of the aortic insufficiency, Sones accidentally entered the right coronary artery with the tip of the cardiac catheter. Before he could remove it, 30 cc of the dye had been released. Sones expected the heart to fibrillate, even go into full arrest, in response to this insult. When it did not, he realized that the coronary arteries could not only tolerate the dye, but that with their aid, he could obtain clear and detailed pictures of coronary circulation in its entirety. As he later said, "I knew that night that we finally had a tool that would divine the anatomic nature of coronary artery disease." Sones went on to perfect his technique, designing special catheters for the purpose and documenting over 1,000 procedures, 95% of which were successful. He presented the procedure to his colleagues in 1962. In the process, he set the stage for future therapeutic interventions such as bypass surgery and, still later, coronary angioplasty.

As the techniques and technology associated with heart disease progressed, advances in pharmaceutical interventions kept pace. One of the major developments of the 1960s was the development of a whole family of drugs called beta blockers (more precisely, adrenergic ß-receptor antagonists) which came out of the laboratory of James Black of Britain. Black initially was seeking a drug to control irregularities of heartbeat, and he tried over 400 analogs before settling on propranolol. Subsequent studies showed that propranolol also lowered blood pressure and the interocular pressure that leads to glaucoma by dilating peripheral nerves. Black received the Mary Lasker Award in 1976 for his pioneering work. Other important heart disease–fighting drugs to come along in these years were the first of the diuretics in 1956; the calcium channel blockers, which became available in 1977; the ACE inhibitors (angiotensin–converting enzyme inhibitors), which were introduced in 1979; the clot-busting streptokinase and TPA (tissue plasminogen activator), which came to market in 1979 and 1987, respectively; and the statins, or cholesterol-reducing drugs, the first of which were approved in 1987. Of a different category of usefulness are the immunosuppressant drugs which are used to discourage heart rejection after transplants. The first really effective immunosuppressant was cyclosporine, developed from fungus, which received FDA approval in 1983.

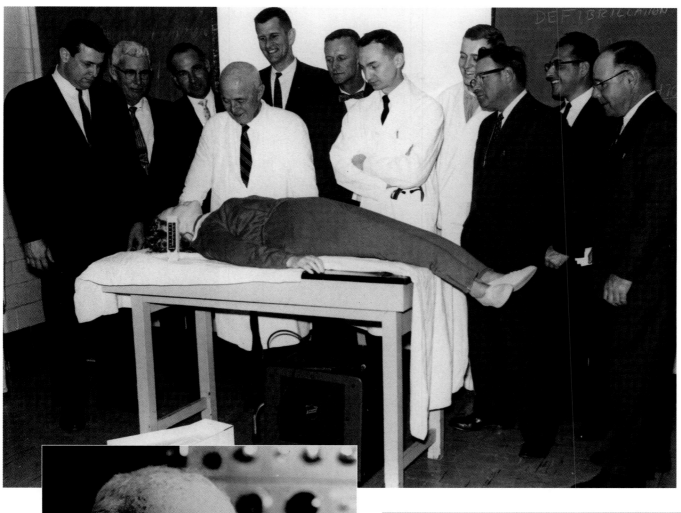

William B. Kouwenhoven's youthful work on the relationship between electrical shocks and the heart back in the 1920s finally bore fruit 30 years later. When he was on staff at a laboratory associated with Johns Hopkins, he was asked by the Edison Electric Institute of New York to design a portable defibrillator for use in resuscitating workmen in the field after severe electrical injury. To this end, Kouwenhoven developed a practical closed-chest instrument—the forerunner of the electrical paddles used by paramedics today—in 1957. Some years later he collaborated with James Jude and Guy Knickerbocker of Johns Hopkins in devising the rhythmic closed-chest compression technique known imprecisely as "heart massage." This procedure, which now includes mouth-to-mouth air support, is the standard procedure for cardiopulmonary resuscitation, practiced all over the world as first aid until an electrical defibrillator can be substituted.

Other names often associated with heart resuscitation include Carl Wiggers and Claude Beck, staff surgeons at Case Western Reserve University Hospital, who combined direct cardiac massage with intravenous injections of adrenaline in the 1940s and taught their techniques to over 3,000 other physicians.

Charles T. Dotter has been called the father of interventional radiology. As a vascular radiologist at the University of Oregon in Portland, Dotter in 1964 had the vision to expand the traditional use of diagnostic angiography to one of nonsurgical angioplasty in peripheral vascular disease. Dotter's specific technique was initially to use a series of catheters of increasing diameter to open blocked arteries and heart valves for the purpose of reshaping vessels and augmenting patients' blood flow. He subsequently modified this method by passing a dilating Teflon sheath over the insertional guide wire and progressively enlarging it until he had achieved an opening of satisfactory size. Dotter's ideas were initially resisted in the United States, but they attracted considerable early interest in Europe. Dotter performed his first percutaneous transluminal angioplasty—of a stenosed femoral artery—in January 1964.

Radiologist Melvin Judkins spent his early professional years at the University of Oregon, where he worked with Charles Dotter in developing and introducing angioplasty. He also studied coronary angiography with Mason Sones at the Cleveland Clinic. Settling finally at Loma Linda Medical Center in California, Judkins went on to create his own system of diagnostic imaging and to perfect the transfemoral approach to selective coronary arteriography as a simpler and safer advance over Sones' brachial artery procedure. Pursuing his lifelong interest in mechanical problems, Judkins also developed a series of specialized catheters, several of which he is shown holding in this 1980 photograph. The Judkins technique of coronary angiography remains the primary diagnostic tool used in catheterization laboratories around the world today.

In 1965, Congress passed, and President Lyndon Johnson signed into law, the Medicare program of national health insurance, securing medical coverage for the elderly and the disabled. At the same time Medicaid, providing medical care to the poor, was enacted. The new laws gave millions of Americans access to low-cost medical treatment for the first time and in the process contributed significantly to the growing demand for heart treatments and to the development of cardiology as a medical specialty. Shown in this photo at the ceremonial signing of the legislation in Independence, Missouri, are Johnson, former President Harry Truman, their wives, and other dignitaries.

The world's first live human heart transplant was completed by Dr. Christiaan Barnard of Capetown, South Africa, in December 1967. Compared in its daring and danger to man's attempts to reach the moon, Barnard's achievement was hailed by the public and many within the medical profession as the dawn of a new age. But the celebrating was somewhat premature. Barnard's first patient, 54-year-old Louis Washkansky, lived 18 days before organ rejection and pneumonia caused his death. Barnard tried again on January 2, 1968, on 58-year-old Philip Blaiberg, who lived 74 days. Almost overnight, 65 other surgical teams in 22 countries attempted to replicate Barnard's tour de force, placing transplanted hearts in 101 patients. But rejection continued to plague the procedure, and five years later only one of the recipients was still alive. Shown in this photograph is Barnard, seated at left, with Michael DeBakey, noted Houston heart surgeon and influential spokesman for cardiology, standing. Also seated is another pioneer in heart transplant research, Dr. Adrian Kantrowitz, Director of Surgical Services, Maimonides Hospital, Brooklyn, New York, who was the first American to attempt a human heart transplant. The gathering marked their joint appearance on the television program "Face the Nation" on December 24, 1967.

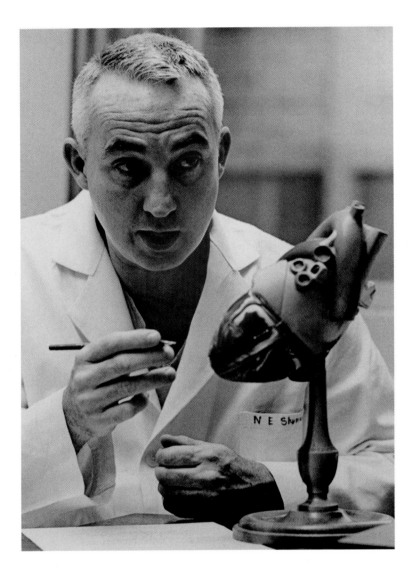

Once heart transplants were shown to be technically feasible, U.S. surgeons were predictably eager to become leaders in the field. Shown here are two distinguished members of the group, Norman Shumway, left, and Denton Cooley, right. Shumway, chief of surgery at Stanford Medical Center, Palo Alto, California, led a team of surgeons in successfully completing the first adult heart transplant in the United States, only days after Barnard's second transplant. Shumway and his Stanford colleagues have also made important contributions in circumventing rejection, devising immune suppressants, and developing an operation for combined heart and lung transplantation, which they successfully performed in 1980. Cooley completed the first successful human heart transplant in the United States in 1968 and a year later became the first heart surgeon to implant an artificial heart in man. Operating at the Texas Heart Institute, located in St. Luke's Episcopal Hospital in Houston, Cooley replaced the diseased heart of Haskell Karp, who lived three days on the temporary assist device while awaiting a human heart. Cooley and his team went on to devise in 1975 the first implantable left ventricular assist device, which was useful in sustaining patients in cardiac failure following open heart surgery, as well as the more advanced HeartMate pump, which is used today by patients awaiting heart transplants. Cooley and his colleagues at the Texas Heart Institute have performed more than 91,000 open-heart operations, reportedly more than any other surgical team in the world. Cooley is noted for his speed as well as his skill; his staff claims that he has sutured transplanted organs into place in as few as 36 minutes.

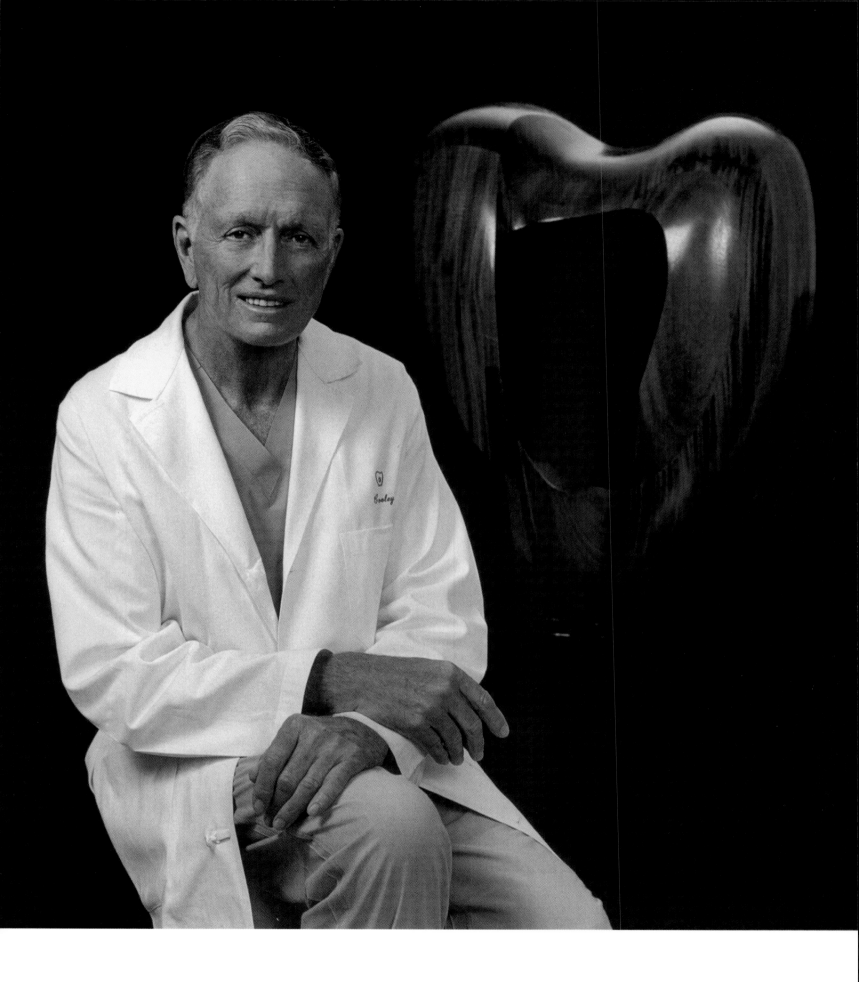

Federal funding for medical care, medical research, and physician training grew dramatically in the 1960s. The field of cardiology was targeted as one of the principal beneficiaries of this expansion, particularly after Lyndon Johnson's 1965 Commission on Heart Disease, Cancer, and Stroke found a "critical shortage" in the number of practicing cardiologists available to treat the aging population. The call to arms was heeded, and by 1973 the number of cardiology training programs had reached 280 with 793 fellows graduating and nearly 1,300 more matriculants in the pipeline in that year alone. Many of the specialists went on to attain board certification and fellowship in the American College of Cardiology, a process that climaxed each year at a formal convocation ceremony. Shown here is one such gathering, held in the 1970s. Ironically, with the changes wrought by managed care in the 1990s, cardiologists found their numbers swelled beyond the market's ability to use all of them to capacity. The training pendulum has since swung back toward having a greater share of heart care handled by internists and primary care physicians.

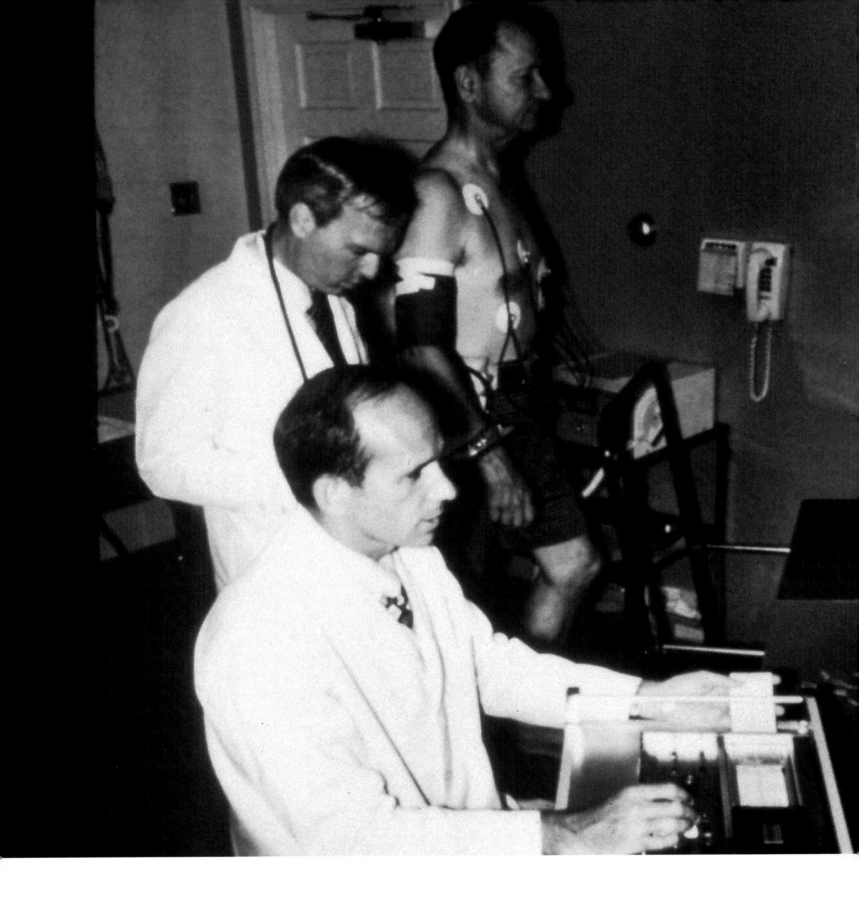

With a background as a specialist in aerospace medicine for the U.S. Air Force and a master's degree in public health medicine as well, Kenneth Cooper, M.D., became convinced in the 1960s that fitness training was a critical tool in helping stem the nation's crisis in heart disease. Apparently, the public found hope in his message too, for when Aerobics, his first book on cardiovascular exercise, was published in 1968, it immediately became a best-seller, and jogging, another part of the Cooper program, became a hugely popular activity. In 1972, shortly before this photo was taken, Cooper left the military to found the Cooper Aerobics Center in Dallas, Texas, from which he has gone on to develop cardiovascular fitness programs for people of all ages and to write a dozen more books on related subjects. Cooper's Institute for Aerobics Research continues to study the relationship of fitness and health as a public health issue. In a study published in 1989 in the Journal of the American Medical Association, Cooper researchers conducting an eight-year study of 13,000 subjects found that those in the bottom 20 percent of fitness ranking were 65 percent more likely to die from heart attacks, strokes, and other chronic diseases than those in the top 20 percent fitness category.

Dr. Cooper was a pioneer in the use of stress ECG or treadmill testing, the diagnostic procedure depicted in the cartoon by Charles Bragg, above. The person being tested is "wired up" to an electrocardiogram and told to walk or run on the motorized treadmill for 20 to 30 minutes while various readings are taken to determine heart efficiency during exertion. The system, which was originally developed for the National Space Program, is widely used in cardiovascular centers today. Another aspect of stress monitoring that dates from the 1950s is the relationship between certain behavior patterns and coronary heart disease. Initially, physiologists detected a statistically higher incidence of coronary heart disease and so-called type-A behavior, which one investigator characterized as "extremes of competitiveness, striving for achievement, restlessness, hyper-alertness, explosive-ness of speech, tenseness of facial musculature, and feelings of being under pressure of time and under the challenge of responsibility." Subsequent studies have narrowed the focus to studying the relationship between "potential for hostility" and heart disease. While nothing conclusive has yet been revealed, the idea that some relationship exists no longer seems in question.

More than a century ago, German biologist Rudolf Virchow found a link between heart disease and cholesterol, but little more was known until the 1980s when scientists at the National Institutes of Health declared triglycerides as markers for lipid conditions that can lead to coronary heart disease. An NIH panel recommended that diet or drugs be used to intervene whenever triglyceride levels exceeded 250 mg/dL, a number soon reduced to 200 mgldL or less. Important distinctions between high-density and low-density lipoproteins have also been drawn in the intervening years, and researchers at NIH continue to refine their dietary recommendations. This NIH photo, part of an early exhibition on cholesterol, cautioned viewers in the accompanying caption that "blood plasma, normally clear, turns milky white when levels of cholesterol and other fatty substances are too high."

Lower Your CHOLESTEROL...

by Making Good Food Choices!

	TRY THESE	INSTEAD OF THESE
Meat, Fish, Poultry and Dried Beans 	Lean beef, lamb, pork, veal, with fat trimmed Poultry without skin Fish Shellfish Dried peas and beans, like split peas, black-eyed peas, chick peas, kidney beans, navy beans, lentils	Fatty cuts of beef, pork, lamb Goose, duck Liver, kidney, brains Sausage, bacon, hot dogs Regular luncheon meats
Dairy Products: Milk and Cheese 	Skim milk, 1% milk, low-fat buttermilk, low-fat evaporated and nonfat dry milk Low-fat soft cheeses, like cottage, farmer, pot Cheeses labeled no more than 2 to 6 grams of fat an ounce Low-fat yogurt	Whole and 2% milk, regular, evaporated, or condensed Cream, half and half, most non-dairy creamers, imitation milk products, whipped cream Cream cheese Hard cheeses Custard style yogurt
Eggs	Egg whites Cholesterol-free egg substitutes	Egg yolks
Fruits and Vegetables 	Fresh, frozen, canned and dried fruits, and vegetables	Vegetables prepared in butter, cream or sauce
Fats and Oils 	Unsaturated vegetable oils: corn, olive, peanut, rapeseed (canola oil), safflower, sesame, soybean Margarine made from unsaturated fats listed above Peanut butter	Saturated fats, like butter, coconut oil, palm oil, palm kernel oil, lard, bacon fat Margarine or shortening made from saturated fats listed above
Breads, Cereals, Pasta and Rice	Sandwich breads Low-fat crackers Hot cereals, most cold dry cereals Noodles and other pasta Rice	Croissants, butter rolls, sweet rolls, Danish pastry, doughnuts, most snack crackers Granola-type cereals made with saturated oils Pasta and rice prepared with cream, butter or cheese sauces; egg noodles
Sweets and Snacks 	Low-fat frozen desserts, like sherbet, sorbet, Italian ice, frozen yogurt, popsicles Low-fat cakes and cookies Low-fat candy, like jelly beans, hard candy Low-fat snacks, like plain popcorn, pretzels Nonfat beverages, like carbonated drinks, juices, tea, coffee	High-fat frozen desserts, like ice cream High-fat cakes, pies and cookies, like most "store-bought" Most candy, like chocolate bars High-fat snacks, like chips, buttered popcorn High-fat beverages, like milkshakes, floats, and eggnogs

"Put Me

On April 15, 1973, more than 900 participants set out to run the 26-mile Boston Marathon. Among the competitors were seven middle-aged heart attack victims from Canada. Calling themselves "the sickest track club in the world," this courageous band from the Toronto Rehabilitation Centre was running to disprove the long-held belief that they and every other person with diagnosed heart disease were ever after condemned to a life of inactivity. Monitored along the route for blood pressure, water loss, and other stress measures by their physician, Dr. Terence Kavanagh, every one of the Torontonians completed the course with no complaints more serious than sore feet. As of 1998, all but one of this stalwart group are alive and well, their ages ranging from 56 to 80. Five continue to exercise regularly, and the youngest finished the same marathon in 1997 in 3 hours, 47 minutes. Their achievement is one of the many positive stories that have helped to change attitudes toward the treatment of heart attack survivors.

Left: To increase public awareness of the dangers of excess cholesterol in the diet, the National Heart, Lung, and Blood Institute set up the National Cholesterol Education Program in 1985, an effort that continues to this day. One medium by which the message is disseminated is through bright, cheery but informative posters like the one shown here.

The first mechanical artificial heart designed to be used as a permanent replacement was designed by Dr. Robert Jarvik of the University of Utah, Salt Lake City, in 1981. Made of polyurethane molded over Dacron mesh, the so-called Jarvik-7 was implanted in the chest of patient Barney Clark by surgeon William DeVries, also of Utah. Clark, who suffered from cardiomyopathy, lived for 112 days before complications in his lungs and kidneys ended his life. The Jarvik-7 and its near-copies were eventually scrapped as impractical. Jarvik's mechanism, for example, was tethered by wires to a cart laden with 375 pounds of machinery, making patient mobility almost impossible. But the idea remains alive. Several fully implantable devices are likely to be ready by the year 2000 as advances in computers and materials technology make mechanical substitutes easier to achieve.

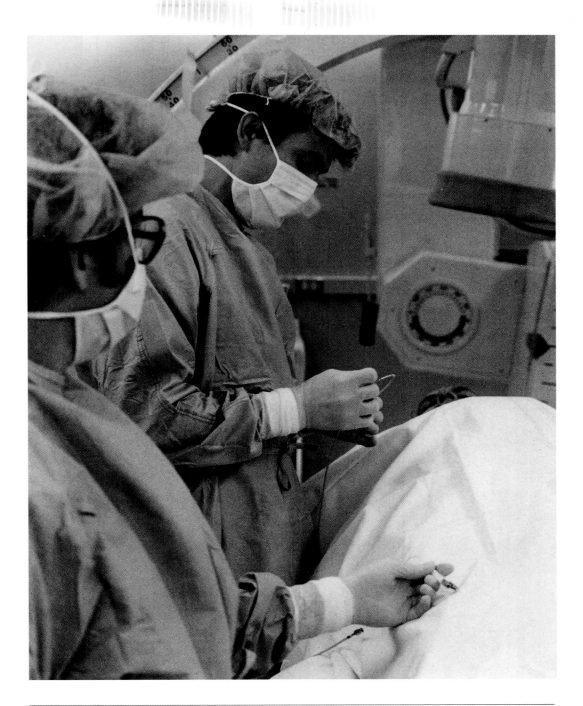

As Charles Dotter's techniques in transluminal angioplasty became known in Europe in the late 1960s, they caught the fancy of Andreas Gruentzig, a young German physician at University Hospital in Zurich. Gruentzig found certain limitations in Dotter's Teflon sheath device, and he began toying with the idea of substituting an inflatable balloon tip to the catheters. In 1975 Gruentzig came up with the solution he had been seeking. Following a series of animal studies, he performed the first percutaneous transluminal coronary angioplasty (PTCA) for the treatment of angina pectoris in 1977. Presenting his findings to the AHA, his technique was first tried in this country by Dr. Richard Myler of Saint Mary's Hospital, San Francisco. Gruentzig went on to offer demonstration courses and to establish a PTCA registry at the National Heart, Lung, and Blood Institute. Cardiologists could now offer some patients a choice between invasive coronary artery bypass graft surgery and noninvasive PTCA with the promise of similar positive results.

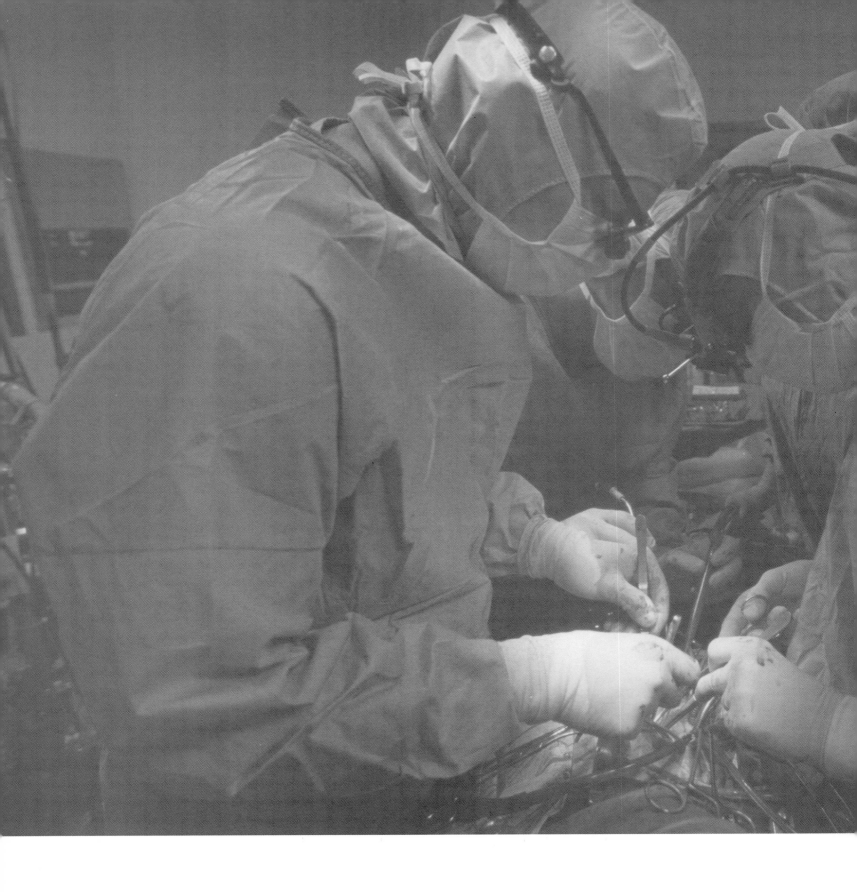

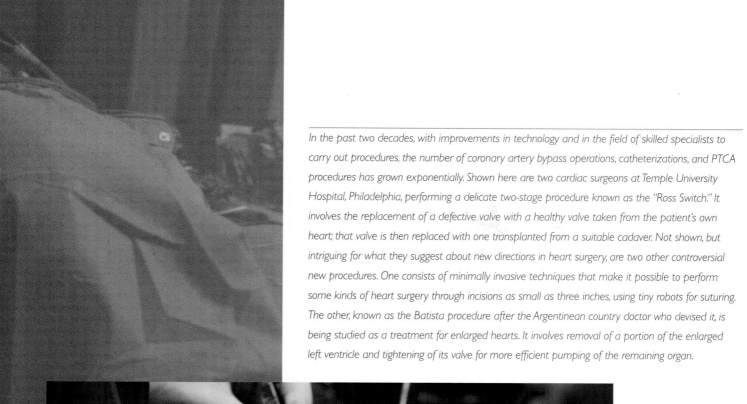

In the past two decades, with improvements in technology and in the field of skilled specialists to carry out procedures, the number of coronary artery bypass operations, catheterizations, and PTCA procedures has grown exponentially. Shown here are two cardiac surgeons at Temple University Hospital, Philadelphia, performing a delicate two-stage procedure known as the "Ross Switch." It involves the replacement of a defective valve with a healthy valve taken from the patient's own heart; that valve is then replaced with one transplanted from a suitable cadaver. Not shown, but intriguing for what they suggest about new directions in heart surgery, are two other controversial new procedures. One consists of minimally invasive techniques that make it possible to perform some kinds of heart surgery through incisions as small as three inches, using tiny robots for suturing. The other, known as the Batista procedure after the Argentinean country doctor who devised it, is being studied as a treatment for enlarged hearts. It involves removal of a portion of the enlarged left ventricle and tightening of its valve for more efficient pumping of the remaining organ.

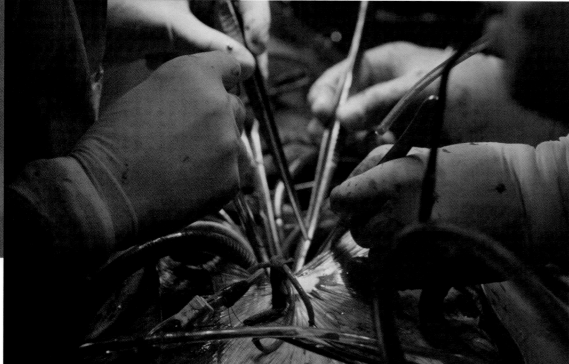

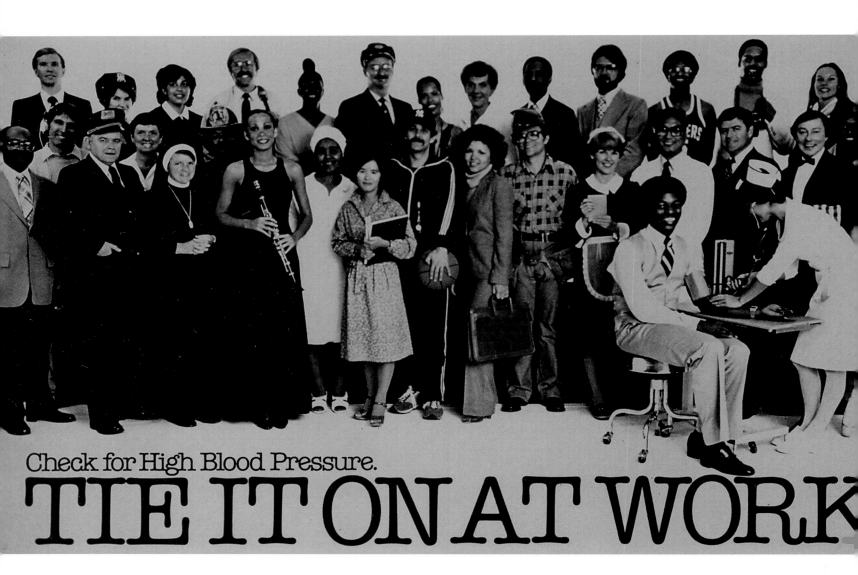

Check for High Blood Pressure.
TIE IT ON AT WORK

Campaigns to make the public more aware of the dangers of high blood pressure were emphasized beginning in 1972 when the National High Blood Pressure Education Program was launched. The NHBPEP was designed as a cooperative effort among professional and voluntary health agencies, as well as local community groups to reduce death and disability related to hypertension. A widely distributed poster campaign and radio and television announcements were designed to reach the public, who were invited to take advantage of low-cost or free screening tests at the grassroots level. The National Heart, Lung, and Blood Institute believes that the effort has paid off. In 1972, less than one quarter of the population polled knew of the relationship between hypertension and heart disease and stroke. Today, three quarters of people surveyed express some knowledge of the subject and most get their blood pressure measured periodically. More significantly, the age-adjusted mortality rate for stroke and coronary heart disease has declined nearly 60 and 53 percent, respectively, improvements attributable in some degree to stepped-up efforts at hypertension control.

So you think you've been cured of high blood pressure

You feel OK . . . your blood pressure reading is normal again. Can you stop taking the high blood pressure pills? No! Most high blood pressure can be *controlled* but not *cured*. If you stop the pills, your blood pressure will go up again. Take your medication. Keep your blood pressure down and under control.

High Blood Pressure... Treat it for Life

Produced by the
National Heart, Lung, and
Blood Institute
for the National High
Blood Pressure Education Program

U.S. DEPARTMENT OF HEALTH AND HUMAN SERVICES
Public Health Service
National Institutes of Health

High blood pressure . . . you can't tell by the way you feel

You can't feel high blood pressure. But some people mistakenly take their high blood pressure medication only when they feel tense, dizzy or have a headache.

Control high blood pressure every day—take your medication regularly.

High Blood Pressure... Treat it for Life

Produced by the
National Heart, Lung, and
Blood Institute
for the National High
Blood Pressure Education Program

U.S. DEPARTMENT OF HEALTH AND HUMAN SERVICES
Public Health Service
National Institutes of Health

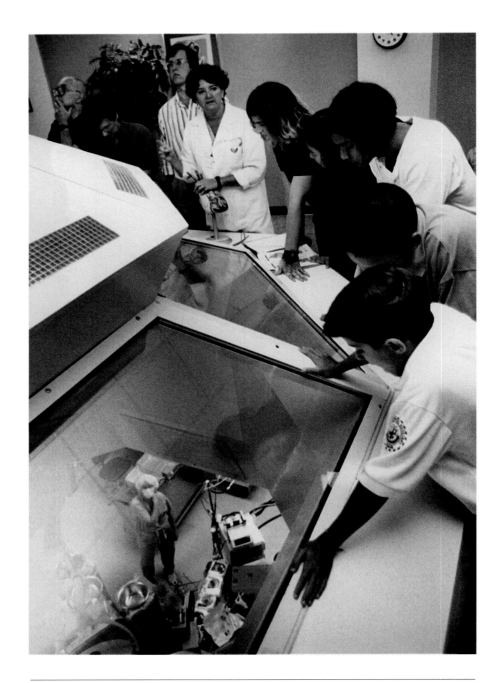

Cardiologists at Fairfax Hospital's Virginia Heart Center believe that one of the most effective ways to make people understand the connection between unhealthy lifestyles and heart disease is to give them a ringside seat at surgical operations. To this end, the hospital opened the Cardiac Observation Dome more than a decade ago. Ever since, surgeons have played to standing-room crowds, many of them high school students on field trips. What visitors get is a shocking view of the consequences of smoking, diets heavy in fat, and lack of exercise on the hearts of adults treated there. And just in case the message is not clear enough, visitors must first file past a table displaying rows of test tubes filled with coagulated fat and labels carrying such information as "8 Ritz® crackers," "1 slice thin-crust pepperoni pizza," and "french fries, small size." A surgical nurse is often standing by to give the play-by-play, too, as surgeons open a patient's chest to reveal coronary arteries clogged with yellowish fatty deposits.

Strategies to Control Atherosclerotic Disease Through Genetics

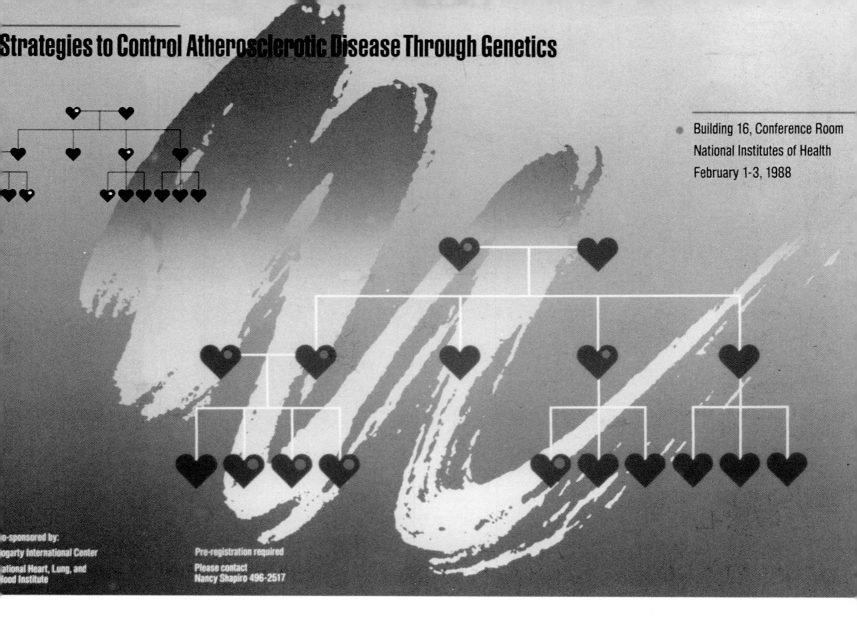

- Building 16, Conference Room
  National Institutes of Health
  February 1-3, 1988

Co-sponsored by:
Fogarty International Center
National Heart, Lung, and
Blood Institute

Pre-registration required
Please contact
Nancy Shapiro 496-2517

Research into the causes and treatments of heart disease increased exponentially in the last two decades of the 20th century. Among the newer areas of exploration are genetics, the subject of the 1988 symposium on Strategies to Control Atherosclerotic Disease Through Genetics announced in this handsome poster. The symposium was held at the NIH's Fogarty Center, so named for the late Congressman John Fogarty of Rhode Island, one of cardiology's staunchest allies before he himself became a victim of heart disease. Research has already gathered a number of important clues to the role of genes in heart disease. One particularly intriguing discovery is that a genetic mutation—dubbed "Apo-A-1 Milano" after the group of villagers in northern Italy who share it—provides near-perfect protection from heart disease. The finding has led to current efforts to synthesize protein and incorporate it into a drug that might reverse atherosclerosis. Two other exciting gene-based investigations were announced at a late-1997 meeting of American heart specialists. The first involves a promising treatment for peripheral vascular disease that uses immature cells containing the genetic code for growth factors that stimulate angiogenesis; injected at locations in the body where blood circulation is blocked, this "biobypass" has restored flow. In the second instance, a gene-based treatment is under study to prevent or delay the common recurrence of blockages in bypass surgery; before grafting, the saphenous vein section is bathed in a solution of genes that naturally block smooth-muscle buildup, with highly favorable results.

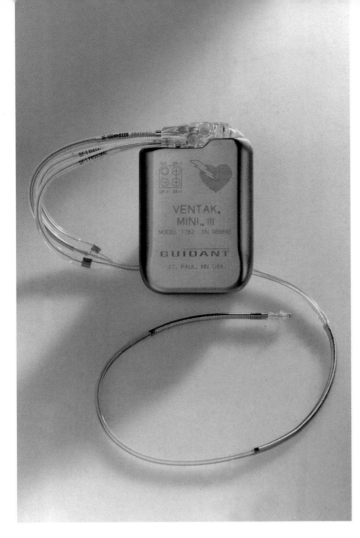

With each passing year, the array of truly remarkable assistive devices available to aid physicians and surgeons in the diagnosis and treatment of heart disorders grows. Each is regulated by the U.S. Food and Drug Administration and must pass rigid FDA tests before entering the market. Some of the more advanced inventions available in 1998 or just over the horizon include those shown on this and the following three pages. At left are two kinds of devices employed in managing cardiac rhythm disturbances. The single unit (top) is an implantable defibrillator, used to treat tachyarrhythmia (hearts that beat excessively at 100 to 200 beats per minute). Uncontrolled rapid heart beat or fibrillation is responsible for an estimated 450,000 sudden death events in the United States each year. A personal defibrillator is typically implanted in a patient's chest or abdomen, and is powered for up to five years by a lithium battery. The group of units shown below left are cardiac pacemakers, generally used to manage bradycardia (fewer than 60 beats a minute as well as other kinds of irregular heartbeat); bradycardia is characterized by symptoms of fatigue, dizziness, and fainting due to inadequate blood flow. Pacemakers work by sending timed electrical impulses to the heart to stimulate and maintain normal rhythm. Newer pacemakers are sensor-driven. They allow the pacemaker to adjust its pacing frequency to match the patient's physical activity level, permitting greater freedom of action.

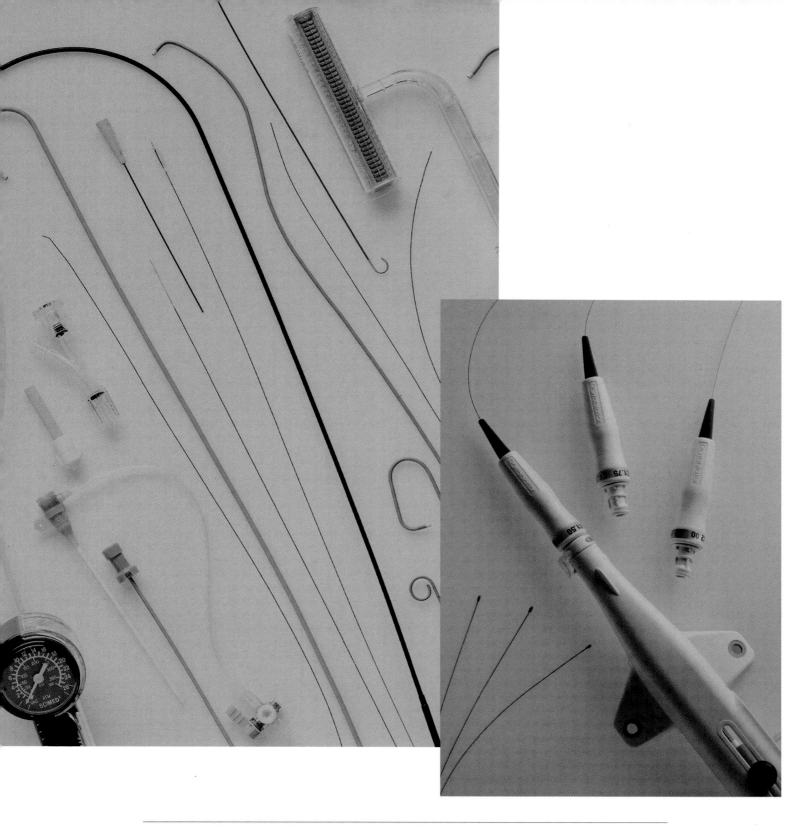

Since the 1970s, many medical heart specialists have opted to perform therapeutic catheterization procedures as less-invasive and less-expensive alternatives to coronary artery bypass graft surgery. Assisting them in this revolution have been a continuous stream of highly refined, miniaturized devices. One such device is the "Roto-Rooter"-like catheter system above right; it performs atherectomies by means of a diamond-tipped burr that rotates within an artery and is driven by a tiny air turbine. A sequence of detachable catheter tips of varying burr size are inserted into the basic power handle, each tip removing a little more plaque in the clogged artery than the one preceding. The atherectomy is completed when sufficient plaque has been removed from the vessel's interior, or lumen, to restore adequate blood flow. Also shown here are an assortment of special-purpose catheters, guide wires, and other state-of-the-art vascular intervention products.

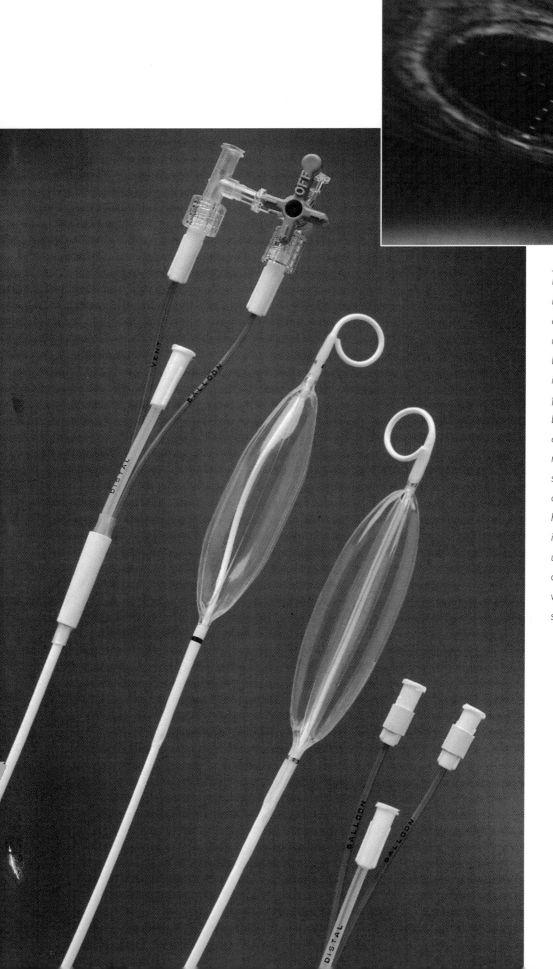

Intravascular ultrasound provides high-resolution imaging of coronary arteries, peripheral vessels, and intracardiac structures. It is used as a diagnostic tool to determine the extent of plaque blockage in arteries. It also aids the cardiologist in determining plaque's consistency—from calcified to soft—critical information that can then be used in selecting the most appropriate therapeutic procedures for the patient. Ultrasound readings are obtained by threading a tiny sound-producing catheter through the arteries and interpreting the echoes produced. Shown here is a typical image of plaque as it appears in cross section on an ultrasound monitor. The unit on which the monitor sits does the actual computation. Devices associated with balloon valvoplasty, the surgical reconstruction of stenosed valves of the heart, are shown at left.

Stents, like that shown greatly enlarged above, are relatively simple expandable devices designed to hold an artery open following withdrawal of an angioplasty balloon. Made of fine lace-like stainless steel wire mesh, of diameters as small as 1mm and in lengths up to 24 mm, stents must be flexible enough for the surgeon to insert in the tiniest and most tortuous locations, yet strong and durable enough to maintain shape and keep the repaired artery open for many years. Stents are deployed to their appointed destinations by a number of means, the most common being the sleeve surrounding a balloon catheter, illustrated at right. Once in place, the balloon inflates to open the vessel and position the stent; the balloon is then deflated and withdrawn leaving the stent behind.

BIBLIOGRAPHY

Acierno LJ. *The History of Cardiology*. London, England: Parthenon Publishing Group; 1994.

Barker WF. *Clio: The Arteries, The Development of Ideas in Arterial Surgery*. Austin, TX: R.G. Landes Co.; 1992.

Bettmann OC. *A Pictorial History of Medicine*. New York, NY: Charles C. Thomas; 1956.

Bruno LC. *The Landmarks of Science*. Washington DC: Library of Congress/Facts on File; 1987.

Comroe JH. *Exploring the Heart, Discoveries in Heart Disease and High Blood Pressure*. New York, NY: W.W. Norton; 1983.

Donahue MP. *Nursing, the Finest Art*. St. Louis, MO: C.V. Mosby; 1985.

Duffy J. *The Healers, A History of American Medicine*. Urbana, IL: University of Chicago Press; 1976.

Eisenberg RL. *Radiology, An Illustrated History*. St. Louis, MO: Mosby Year Book; 1992.

Flaste R. *Medicine's Great Journey, One Hundred Years of Healing*. Boston, MA: Little, Brown & Co.; 1992.

Fye WB. *American Cardiology, The History of a Specialty and Its College*. Baltimore, MD: The Johns Hopkins University Press; 1996.

Garrison FH. *An Introduction to the History of Medicine*. Philadelphia, PA: W.B. Saunders Co.; 1929.

Goldin G. *Work of Mercy, A Pictorial History of Hospitals.* Ontario, Canada: The Boston Mills Press; 1994.

Hackett E. *Blood, The Biology, Pathology, and Mythology.* New York, NY: Saturday Review Press; 1973.

Lyons AS, Petrucelli, II RJ. *Medicine, An Illustrated History.* New York, NY: Abradale Press & Harry N. Abrams; 1987.

McGrew RE. *Encyclopedia of Medical History.* New York, NY: McGraw-Hill; 1985.

Novotny A, Smith C. *Images of Healing.* New York, NY: Macmillan; 1980.

Rowbottom M, Susskind C. *Electricity and Medicine: History of Their Interaction.* San Francisco, CA: San Francisco Press; 1984.

Rutkow IM. *Surgery: An Illustrated History.* St. Louis, MO: Mosby Year Book Inc.; 1993.

Williams G. *The Age of Agony, The Art of Healing, 1700-1800.* Chicago, IL: Academy Publishers; 1986.

Williams G. *The Age of Miracles, Medicine and Surgery in the Nineteenth Century.* Chicago, IL: Academy Publishers; 1987.

Photo Credits

American College of Cardiology, Bethesda, MD—182-183

American Heart Association, Dallas, TX—147

Bakken Library and Museum, Minneapolis, MN—43 (top), 50, 58, 59, 85, 137

Bayer Corporation, Morristown, NJ—68 (bottom), 97

Boston Scientific Corporation, Boston, MA—161 (top), 163, 199, 200, 201

Chesney Medical Archives, Johns Hopkins University, Baltimore, MD. Allen Mason, photographer—153

Cleveland Clinic Archives, Cleveland, OH. Yu Kwan Lee, photographer—161 (bottom), 173

Cooper Aerobics Center, Dallas, TX—184, 185

Corbis-Bettmann, New York, NY—cover, 60, 150

Corbis-Bettmann, New York, NY. Leif Skoogfors, photographer—192, 193

Corbis-Bettmann, New York, NY. Baldwin H. Ward, photographer—61

Charles Dotter Memorial Research Laboratory for Interventional Radiology, Oregon Health Sciences Library, Portland, OR—176

Emory University School of Medicine, Atlanta, GA—191

Framingham Heart Study, Framingham, MA—156, 157

W. Bruce Fye Collection, Minneapolis, MN—99, 129, 130, 132, 133

Guidant Corporation, St. Paul, MN—198

Harvard Medical Library in the Francis A. Countway Library of Medicine, Boston, MA—117, 146-147

William H. Helfand Collection, New York, NY—96

Historical Museum of Medicine and Dentistry, Hartford Medical Society, Hartford, CT—107

Herbert Hoover Presidential Library, West Branch, IA—148-149

Inova Health System, Fairfax, VA. Ann Doyle, photographer—196

Eileen Judkins, Loma Linda University, Loma Linda, CA. Robert Rearick, photographer—177

LBJ Library Collection, Austin, TX—178

Library of Congress, Washington, DC—26, 27 (background), 57, 116

Maryland Historical Society, Prints and Photographs Division, Baltimore, MD—cover, 2-3, 101 (bottom), 112-113

Mayo Clinic, Rochester, MN—170, 171

Medtronic, Inc., Minneapolis, MN—166, 167, 168, 169

Menczer Museum of Medicine and Dentistry, Hartford, CT—101 (top), 107

Minnesota Historical Society, St. Paul, MN—144-145

Mütter Museum, Philadelphia College of Physicians, Philadelphia, PA—66, 67, 134-135

New York Academy of Medicine, New York, NY—80, 81

Rockefeller Archive Center, North Tarrytown, NY—149

Rockefeller University Archives, New York, NY—151

Rush-Presbyterian–St. Luke's Medical Center Archives, Chicago, IL—136

St. Luke's Hospital, Kansas City, KS—172

Texas Heart Institute, Houston, TX—181

Toronto Rehabilitation Centre, Toronto, Canada—189

UPI/Corbis-Bettmann, New York, NY—179, 180, 190

Western History Collections, University of Oklahoma Library, Oklahoma City, OK—135

All other photographs courtesy of the National Library of Medicine, Bethesda, MD.

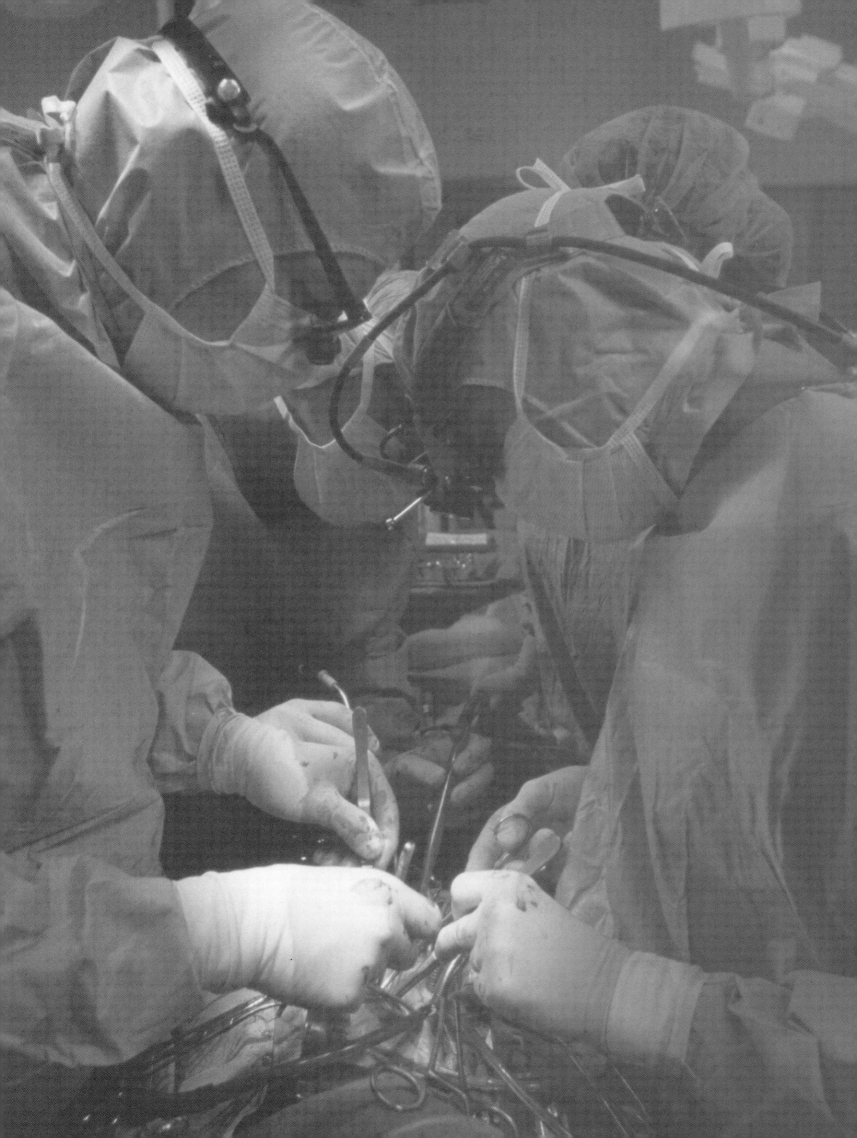